EMMA STOTT

SPEEDY READING

Fast Strategies for Teaching
GCSE English Literature Post-Lockdown

First published 2020

by John Catt Educational Ltd,
15 Riduna Park, Station Road,
Melton, Woodbridge IP12 1QT

Tel: +44 (0) 1394 389850
Email: enquiries@johncatt.com
Website: www.johncatt.com

ISBN: 978 1 913622 28 2

Set and designed by John Catt Educational Limited

REVIEWS

Emma's passion and enthusiasm for her subject is clearly evident in this exceptionally pragmatic guide. She sets out highly efficient methods teachers of literature can adopt in order to teach to the top, regardless of the prior attainment of their students. Her strategies are aspirational, practical and above all have the desire to inspire an appreciation of the power of literature at their heart. A must for any teacher of literature feeling overwhelmed at the sheer volume of content to be covered on the course.

Kathrine Mortimore,
Lead practitioner for English at Torquay Academy

This is a highly engaging, highly useful and well-researched book for English teachers. The author reflects intelligently on her own teaching and on how she has developed and refined this through her experience in the classroom as well by testing her approaches against key thinking in the field. Stott manages to boil her experience and research down to just a handful of key areas and key ideas that will help even the most experienced and skilled of teachers improve their practice. Especially useful is the idea that rather than worry about pupils learning huge amounts of details about texts, English teachers can focus on teaching explicit concepts about how all texts work.

Neil Bowen,
English teacher, author and consultant

CONTENTS

For my first teachers: Mum, Dad and Nanna, with love.
And for my current teachers – my students.
Thank you.

INTRODUCTION

The demands of the English Literature exams have always been burdensome: an anthology of poetry, a play by Shakespeare, 19th-century prose, modern fiction, and unseen texts. And then this all needs to dovetail with the rigours of the Language papers. Before Covid-19, it was a big request. Now it feels like an impossible labour.

But as teachers, minor miracles are our stock in trade. Teaching has always been about accelerating learning, developing critical thinking and mastering exam skills; we're already experts on this.

We now need to pause and gather together the *most* effective methods, but alongside this we also have to consider some new approaches. In the past we've had to work with students with poor attendance, so we can draw on this; we've had to teach students who arrive knowing little English, so we can use this too. Although our situation is strange, we've prepared for parts of it for *years*.

As someone who's taught English in a disadvantaged area, I know schools provide much more than 'core content' or GCSE grades for students. When school closures were mentioned in March 2020, I kept thinking: how was I going to be able to provide emotional support to my students, whilst still keeping their learning up to date? When lockdown was eventually imposed, my school responded rapidly, organising virtual lessons, designing learning packs and providing research-based training on how to engage students remotely, but like many teachers I was still deeply worried about learners keeping up. And even more worried about how we could best support them when they returned to school.

But this changed when I realised that I'd felt this way before. Occasionally, it's seemed as if some of my students have missed *years* of schooling. Many of the students I'd instructed before needed to catch up. I've even taught phonics strategies to KS4 students, who still went on to achieve at GCSE level. Once I realised that the situation wasn't as unknown as I'd first thought, it made me think instead: how have I tried to get through this before? How *have* I got through this before? What's helped my students to triumph even though the odds were against them? And how have I been able to build relationships and provide emotional support despite having so much content to teach?

Fortunately, I previously taught early entry GCSE Literature to ease the load on SEND and LPA students. I must say that these students were an inspiration to me – despite educational and personal challenges, they showed determination, courage and insight. If those students could take it in their stride that they were going to complete an exam in half the time of most other learners, then I needed to get my act together!

Through teaching early entry, I gathered numerous methods for condensing the content and knew that this actually *increased* attainment for many of my learners. I looked back at those schemes of work and began to develop them with students of all abilities in mind. I scoured my notebooks and pulled out any glimmer of potential. I delved into folders of research, as I'm lucky enough to be part of an EEF Research School. Sometimes, I tried out these ideas with my classes remotely. The fastest progress was made with two newer methods: Labov's narrative model and Frank Kermode's matrix. I began to feel in control of the situation.

Now I want to help other educators feel this way. This book contains everything I've found effective in establishing strong comprehension, robust recall, acceleration and elaboration. The strategies have been created in response to research on literacy, metacognition and memory in particular, and from my findings as a research facilitator specialising in challenge in a Research School.

The strategies have been used with low prior attainment (LPA) and high prior attainment (HPA) students with adjustments, but I also know that the students doomed to be thought of as LPA are much more capable than we often allow them to be. I've found 'teaching to the top' to be an invaluable guide in itself. Many of the strategies for challenge have come from my work with those supposedly lower ability groups, who often have the most original inferences. Whilst differentiation is important, these strategies don't need to change too much. Prior attainment is *not* current ability. Let's think more of what we can achieve in the present.

Whilst the primary focus for these strategies is the GCSE English Literature exam – it's arguably more taxing in terms of content – nevertheless, they'll work for the Language exam too. The longer I teach, the more I'm interested in strategies that work across language and literature. I've begun to think of some of the older approaches as single-use plastic – only if I can rinse and recycle do I now want to embed the pedagogy.

Admittedly, some of the strategies are shortcuts, and I would prefer a system where students don't have to give an impression of the skill but have time to become truly skilful. But they are a compromise to help our learners progress to the next level of their education and their lives. They can also permit us to spend time on more important things, like providing emotional support. Helpful quick fixes sometimes exist!

This book presents eight strategies that help students to speedily learn the content of the GCSE texts and the significant language and defining 'big ideas' around them, whilst also keeping an eye on how to write about these. As the Assessment Objectives of each of the exam boards mostly align, all the strategies are created to increase AO1 (inference), AO2 (language analysis), AO3 (contextual awareness), and AO4 (spelling, punctuation and grammar). They're not gimmicks, but reliable and replicable strategies that should still be useful once we've got back to 'normal'.

OVERVIEW OF THE STRATEGIES

1. **Reading is Rebellion**. How can we make reading fascinating? We make it dangerous! I'll outline how to increase engagement with literature itself.

2. **Cold and Hot Reading**. I'll proceed with some ideas on general reading skills. Teaching students methods for first and closer reads equips them for any exam, but also shows that without

having studied say an entire anthology of poetry, they can write meaningfully about any of them.

3.   **The Matrix.** This idea, borrowed from the inestimable Frank Kermode, shows how text can be reduced without reducing critical appreciation. I'll develop this idea into a more stranded approach linked to the assessment objectives, taking the focus off plot and quotation recall and on to richer inferences and skilful analytical writing.

4.   **Buzzwords.** This strategy looks at the high-leverage language that our students can learn in order to think and write critically about literature.

5.   **The Big Five.** Instead of learning endless technical terms, five can be taught that are multi-purpose.

6.   **Spaced Learning.** This is a well-researched method for supporting the rapid input and memorisation of content.

7.   **Metacognition is Your Friend.** I'll look at ways to make the teaching of the previous strategies as embedded, effective (and effortless) as possible.

8.   **Analogy is All.** It's my contention that an understanding of analogy *is* an understanding of literature. I'll explain the importance of explicating metaphorical imagery – *the* close reading skill.

The final chapter in the book is a quick fix 'trouble-shooter', which summarises common problems in teaching English GCSE and the quick fixes or strategies that can help to solve them. This is followed by a glossary of general terms, an appendix that reduces some of the set poems down to three or four matrices, and an appendix that outlines a suggested timetable for how to teach the strategies for the first time.

I hope the strategies help you as much as they have helped me.

STRATEGY 1: READING IS REBELLION

WHAT?

Books are incendiary devices; books are dangerous. At least two of the set texts I teach would be given an 18 certificate if they were a film or video game.

But we make them seem safe. Cosy. *Quiet.*

Extraordinarily, the GCSE set texts are some of the most seditious. We need to exploit this. It may seem too late to try to 'sell' reading in this way by the time we reach the exam, but we can strive to make students feel they are part of a dialogue that many in society don't want them to contribute to. And despite the efforts of governments and mark schemes, the set texts haven't been entirely neutered.

Every time students interpret, they pull out the pin and let another idea, argument or thought explode. Literature is loud! Even the mildest texts contain 'taboos': Humpty Dumpty reveals that the armed forces are ineffectual; Baa Baa Black Sheep dares to empower children economically; Hey Diddle Diddle celebrates mixed relationships. Exciting, yes?

Progress is slowed by cautious, ponderous approaches to the text. Bounce into the room as if you've never read the text before, let alone taught it. You need to appear exhilarated and even nervous about teaching the text. Furthermore, this reminds you that the prose or poem is new to your students and prevents those accidental slips where we forget that they haven't also read the text 50 times before.

Make students aware that reading is rebellion. Through texts, they can question and explore ideas; they can challenge authority.

So, rid them of the misconception that the text is an authority to be respected. It isn't. It's a matrix where the subversive originates and fizzes.

Numbers behave themselves, but words don't. Make it thrilling that language obfuscates, confuses and puzzles. It damn well should!

This isn't as fast to fix as some of the strategies, but it should twinkle behind your delivery of the others. Nothing gets students' ears straining like 'Many people find this book offensive', 'Some school libraries banned this book', or 'I once got a letter from an angry parent because of teaching this book.'

HOW?

It might seem cheap, but swearing engages. I'll concede it's controversial, but taboo language is part of the set texts. The government says we should teach it! And any word, however offensive, has played a part in our wider discourse, so we can't just ignore it.

I've galvanised bored groups by focusing on expletives in texts. A reliable source has been Philip Larkin's 'This Be the Verse'. Interestingly, many students don't find the language as scandalous as the criticism of parents. Or the staid image of Larkin himself compared to the rancour of the poem. Straightaway, this poem shows literature is *not safe*.

We often want our students to 'develop a love of reading'. I'm not sure I want this. Firstly, you can't force love, and you can't teach love. Secondly, I'm not certain I *love* reading. Reading is an obsession, something I'm driven to do because I can't kick the habit of knowledge. Sometimes, I loathe reading. I choke on the injustice, cant and ignorance that literacy makes me aware of. I certainly don't want to *cuddle* much of what I read. Students don't have to love it; I want them to be excited and agitated by reading. If we really have to, we could say to be 'in love' with reading. It's a much more restless state!

After exposure to a controversial text, I like to twist the controversy. With Larkin, I show my students a poll of the most offensive words in English, where predictably the F word reigns high. We then challenge this. Why is the N word not the most offensive? Why is a word that's ultimately about procreation rather than destruction perceived with disgust?

Students are being made aware that texts aren't agreeable and that texts can make us squirm.

I like to increase the crackle in the room by crossing out words in the poem's first line: 'They fuck you up your mum and dad.' I put a big black mark through 'mum and dad' and write teachers.

This can then be linked to the idea that the text itself is the best teacher in the room; texts are superior educators and full of lessons about forbidden things.

Although time is stretched, by discussing at least one controversial text per half term, you can maintain a sizzle in the classroom. When students feel they have a stake in literature – that is, when they perceive it is concerned with the things that concern them – they will learn better. Research from the Ambition Institute helps to inform how we can 'catalyse' learning. In their invaluable report *Learning: What Is It, and How Might We Catalyse It?*, Peps Mccrea explains that students attend better to things that they value.[1] The more we attend, the more we learn, and we only learn what we attend to. Students are more likely to value literature if it's presented to them as a force of change, protest and rebellion.

Controversies abound in the set texts, helping us to maintain the idea that literature is radical. I always allocate a lesson to *Macbeth's* Porter scene (Act 2, Scene 3).[2] It's not a cheap shot – the failings of sex and the condemnation of equivocation are central themes of the play. But I won't deny that explicating dirty jokes perks up the wearied scholar!

---

1. Mccrea, P. (2019) *Learning: What Is It and How Might We Catalyse It?* Ambition Institute.
2. This scene is often viewed as comic relief but is an insight into Macbeth's despair at the failings of his masculinity. The Porter makes jokes about sexual inadequacy but, crucially, makes apparent that equivocators won't be admitted to heaven. This is a handy idea for the literary scholar – we can always maintain that Macbeth is difficult to define and explicate because it is crammed with equivocation!

TARGET PRACTICE

We can encourage iconoclasm when our students read. What ideology is the author criticising? Let's hoist that idea and see how the writer uses language to knock it down. Which missiles (criticisms) are strongest? Does the idea manage to stand solid throughout the barrage? Or does the writer bludgeon it flat? Show students that words are destructive as well as creative. I call this technique 'Target practice'. Figure 1 shows an example from *An Inspector Calls*.[3]

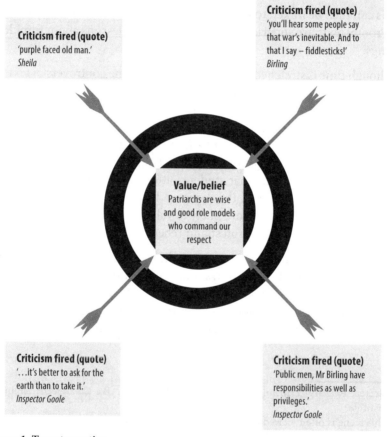

Criticism fired (quote)
'you'll hear some people say that war's inevitable. And to that I say – fiddlesticks!'
Birling

Criticism fired (quote)
'purple faced old man.'
Sheila

Value/belief
Patriarchs are wise and good role models who command our respect

Criticism fired (quote)
'...it's better to ask for the earth than to take it.'
Inspector Goole

Criticism fired (quote)
'Public men, Mr Birling have responsibilities as well as privileges.'
Inspector Goole

Figure 1: Target practice

---

3. Priestly, J. B. (1992) *An Inspector Calls*. Oxford: Heinemann.

By using the template in Figure 1, students are forced to explicate the quotes in terms of how they link to a central argument. This means their commentary is going to be on bigger ideas (aka context), rather than simple paraphrasing of quotations.

I most often employ this technique once students have a sound knowledge of plot and characters; it's been an effective method to prepare students for their first essay on the text. But students can also be introduced to a text by giving them a key value and a limited number of quotations (criticisms) before they begin to read it.

I once had a very bright class who despised Dickens. This was partly my fault – I'd causally mentioned his infidelity in a previous lesson and they never forgot it! Some students also thought *A Christmas Carol* was rather childish. To overcome this, I began with the value that sex is an entirely private matter. I gave them a list of quotations showing the effects of Scrooge's apathy and greed, and some quotations showing the joy of family life. I'll admit this isn't a theme that will appear on the exam paper, but it's definitely not childish! Students began to argue that Dickens was making us aware that sex, or rather procreation, is not private as it's society's duty to care for children. This then lead to a discussion about overpopulation and then a rhetorical piece on the topic in a later lesson. I can't say my students became Dickens fans but grumbles about the novella certainly stopped!

To use the 'Target practice' technique, consider beginning with a class discussion on the dominant values in the text and collect these on the board. Make sure students are aware that values are themes, i.e. recurring ideas in the text. As a class you can then choose the most important values/themes, before settling on one value to explore thoroughly.

Provide students with a quotation bank to guide them in their choices when they begin to match quotes to the value. (I don't discourage my students from finding their own quotes, but working with a limited number is usually more effective.) I usually choose a quotation first and narrate the 'attack' it's making on the value. Students can then work independently on completing their copy of the diagram, before coming together as a class to discuss which quotations are the sharpest 'arrows'.

For example, one student might suggest that Birling underestimating the threat of war highlights his lack of foresight, meaning patriarchs are not inherently wise. Another student might propose that Birling's belief the Titanic is 'unsinkable' is indicative of arrogance and therefore he should not be respected. To stretch students, try countering their inferences. For instance, I might argue that Birling is a man who's kept himself up to date with current affairs and, in fact, alludes to the present more than his children. Doesn't this show he's at least wiser than others in the family? Students can then look again at their original quotation to see if they can wring any more inferences out of it, or can move on to another quotation that attacks the value. This helps students to reduce the text to its richest quotes.

The diagram can then be extended by asking what type of 'arrow' is being fired (e.g. metaphor) to link the analysis back to language features. For example, students might discuss the irony of Birling's comments, his dismissive phrase 'some people', or the unequivocal adjective 'unsinkable'. Does this technique strengthen the writer's criticism? Now students have to be judicious in identifying and explaining the most telling techniques.

Next you can look at the value the diagram has explicated and create an exam question around it. The value 'patriarchs are wise and good role models who command our respect' might become: 'How does Priestley present the character of Birling?' or 'How does Priestley use the family unit to explore societal values?' Eventually, students can create their own questions based on the values.

I've found the diagrams have been great at getting students to 'own' their essays from beginning to end. I also like this technique because it can be used later on as a visual organiser and revision method. However, don't forget that the initial time this technique is used, the point of it should be to show that texts are iconoclastic. Don't worry if the first time students use the technique, the lesson is more discussion-based. Get students to care about the values/themes first and they're more likely to care about the text.

COMING SOON

Anticipation can also be leveraged to raise engagement and to help students make connections across different texts. For the first lesson, I like to make a 'coming soon' advert that frames the texts in contentious ways. In the example in Figure 2, I've also included auxiliary texts that link to the key themes of set texts.

The Gay Science
God is dead!
Debate Friedrich Nietzsche's controversial argument

Checking out Me History
John Agard
Dead white males – who needs them?

Dr Faustus
Christopher Marlowe
Satanic Panic!
Find out who is willing to make a deal with death, danger and the devil…

COMING SOON!

The Applicant
Sylvia Plath
'First, are you our sort of a person?
Do you wear a glass eye, false teeth or a crutch, a brace or a hook, rubber breasts or a rubber crotch, stitches to show something's missing? No, no?
Then how can we give you a thing?
Stop crying. Open your hand. Empty?
Empty. Here is a hand.'

The Wanting seed
Anthony Burgess
Imagine an overpopulated society. Imagine you are have to be gay by law. What sacrifice will you make for the next generations?

DNA
Dennis Kelly
It is in our DNA to brutalise and butcher; it is in our DNA to cooperate

Figure 2: Coming soon advert

REBELLIOUS THEMES TO EXPLORE IN THE GCSE SET TEXTS

Below are a few examples of the more contentious (and often neglected) passages that you could explore in the GCSE set texts.

DNA: Many teachers skim over Leah's notorious monologue that describes the sexual practices of bonobos. However, this can be read as an allegory of the sex and death drive, or the dichotomy between the human needs to create and destroy. I often explain to my students that I'm uncomfortable reading out the line 'They shag a lot', yet I don't feel this when reading out the characters' descriptions of the torture and murder of Adam. What does this say about me? What does this say about our society? Why does sex appal more than violence?

Frankenstein: Most discussions of the creature's threat that 'I will be with you on your wedding night' usually focus on how Frankenstein believes he (rather than his wife) is in danger, hinting further at his hubris. Whilst this a sound reading, we could look at the creature as a manifestation of Frankenstein's hidden desires. What if Frankenstein chooses to leave his bride on their wedding night because he does not want to consummate the marriage? Or he fears he will treat his bride monstrously, thereby meaning the monster is with him? Does the creature want to ensure that Frankenstein can have no more 'children'? Whereas *DNA* and *A Christmas Carol* portray sex (or its results) as optimistic, this novel seems to present procreation as bleak and destructive. We could also re-examine the ending of the novel, when the creature walks off to his death after the death of his creator. Does this image imply God himself is dead to us?

Othello: An intriguing way to open up debate about the treatment of women in this play is to gather Iago's and Othello's quotations about Desdemona. Juxtapose Othello's 'prove my love a whore' with Iago's 'an old black ram is tupping your white ewe'. Before your students know anything about the play, ask them what this reveals about the speaker. Do they think the same person said this? Why? What prejudices might these quotes reveal? It's surprising how Iago and Othello are revealed to share a misogynistic view, and it shocks students when they encounter the noble Othello in the first part of the play. Does one prejudice breed another? Does being the victim of prejudice make you more or less likely to be prejudiced?

Twelfth Night: Rarely is much time spent on the sly 'by my life, this is my lady's hand: these be her very C's, her U's, and her T's; and thus makes she her great P's.' Malvolio reads this innuendo (essentially spelling out the C word) aloud when he receives the trick letter. Giggles are guaranteed (once the joke's pointed out), but typically for Shakespeare, the crux of the play is smuggled in the smut. This quotation is really a summing up of the plot and a reveal of its key theme. Like with the Porter scene, if students understand this quote, then they understand *Twelfth Night*.

Malvolio is unaware of the joke, similar to many of our students at first, so how can we be sure we're never figures of ridicule? Furthermore, the Cs etc. lead to the great Ps. That is, the letter and the play are 'taking the piss' out of pomposity. However self-assured and self-important we are, our values can be lampooned. What's more, authority can be mimicked, so can we really trust it?

A Christmas Carol: Whilst these may not exactly be controversial parts of the novella, I find them underexplored. Firstly, how significant is it that Scrooge has a head cold? Does this mean he has a temperature and has therefore hallucinated the visitations? Does this matter? Does it mean that Scrooge's deepest desire is redemption and he is really the agent of his own deliverance? Can we read the text secularly? Is the title merely commercial? Dickens' Christian faith is often overemphasised, so taking a non-religious view of the text can be enlightening. Also, why does Scrooge's father change? Has he been visited by ghosts? Does this doom Fred or even mean that Scrooge's 'adopted son' Tiny Tim will also sour?

WHY?

I'm a teacher first and foremost because I'm besotted by words and linguistic theory. It's perhaps controversial to say that this is my first motivation above wanting to help young people to achieve, but I want them to achieve *through the medium* I hold dearest. Subject knowledge appears to have slipped down the chain of desirable teacher qualities, but a truly erudite and fervent teacher will always ignite excitement. It really can't be faked, so if you're feeling frustrated by set texts, you need to see them as protests. I want to help make the world better, so I'm a teacher (of the protest!), but I also need my discipline to thrive, and the next generation has to value the subject and be allowed to be its gatekeepers. I've seen some teachers almost appear to resent giving students the most powerful knowledge. I hear 'that's A level' or 'that's degree content', as if we should be bouncers on the doors of scholarship! We must make sure that students are equipped to know more than us eventually. That starts with them valuing, not loving, text.

Make reading radical. Imagine the books on your classroom shelves are Chekov's gun: he said you should never have a gun in a narrative if it won't be fired. Well, those books shouldn't just be stage dressing; they must be fired. When you first meet a class, hold a book to you ear and explain you can hear it ticking like a bomb. The plot twist, the taboo language, the bold criticism can go BANG! at any time. If you're not keen on this image, try the volcano that lies dormant and then...

But if our students aren't confident readers, none of this fanfare will help directly. We need to make reading rebellious, but at the same time make students aware that reading is not only a taboo-breaking act, but a code-breaking one. Our second strategy – 'Cold and hot reading' – lets our students 'hack the system'.

Strategy 1: Reading is rebellion		
What?	**How?**	**Why?**
• Make reading seem **dangerous** and forbidden. • Create **anticipation** about texts.	• Exhibit the book as a 'ticking bomb'. • Advertise the book with a '**coming soon**' poster. • Begin with the **most controversial** parts of the text. • Apply the **target practice** method of analysis.	• Text is a force for social change (both good and bad), therefore it's truly dangerous. • Students need to value, rather than love, reading. Students must understand why text is worth the time to decode.

STRATEGY 2: COLD AND HOT READING

We know that robust reading skills must be embedded before knowledge of the set texts can be mastered – but also that the reality is often different. Those of us who've taught LPA students (actually, students of all abilities) know that we frequently have to teach shortcuts to reading and comprehension; many of us suffer guilt at the little tips and tricks we instil to create an *illusion* of reading. I certainly felt this way before I found that 'cold and hot' reading is a very effective way to mitigate this.

The reading process works on a continuum:

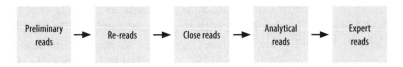

Figure 3: The reading continuum

This diagram can be used to illustrate to students that the reading process is never complete and that different strategies will be required at different points on the continuum.

Many students begin to analyse the text before they have an initial understanding of it; other students hate re-reading, finding it unnecessarily repetitive. The continuum shows how each step must be secure before the student can progress, and that most extracts need to be read at least four times to even approach a worthy level of understanding.

'Cold' reading occurs early in the process, becoming 'hot' reading further along the continuum.

The continuum allows us to build on Doug Lemov's advice to 'name the steps'.[4] We can direct students to 'name steps' that help with a preliminary read and then enquire how the steps might be different when we begin to close read. It's effective to display the continuum on the board when approaching texts with students – either shorter extracts or whole novels – and students can suggest strategies for whichever part of the continuum the lesson will be focusing on. For instance, if we're looking again at the prologue in *Romeo and Juliet*, I'll ask where we are on the continuum and what strategies will best serve us that day.

'Cold' reading relies on some common-sense approaches that can be applied to any text, whilst 'hot' reading relies on more specific background knowledge. Teaching our students the difference is a great first step to overcoming literacy barriers. The research gathered in *What Works* shows that explicit teaching of reading comprehension strategies can help a student progress by six months.[5] However, the research also suggests that using the same strategies too often is detrimental: strategies have to develop with a student's skills and should become progressively more challenging. I developed cold and hot reading in response to this and linked them to the reading continuum so I had a menu of methods that increased in complexity. This also makes it clear to students that their methodology will develop along with their understanding. That is, skills and knowledge will grow together. This helps to prevent the situation where students have a great knowledge of a text but lack the skills to unify the knowledge effectively.

COLD READING: WHAT?

Cold reading means reading a text the student hasn't seen before and comprehending the explicit content. Before moving on to a closer look at language and implicit content (hot reading), students can make some general predictions about the text. For instance, most texts will satisfy

---

4. Lemov, D. (2015) *Teach Like a Champion*. San Francisco: Josey Bass.
5. Major, L. E. and Higgins, S. (2019) *What Works*. London: Bloomsbury.

the criteria of Labov's narrative model;[6] consequently, students will know to look for answers to what, who, where and when.

They will also be primed to search for conflicts and problems, and any changes from the beginning to the end of the text. Essentially, they will understand the (predictable) code of literature.

COLD READING: WHY?

Students are often left mystified by the reading process. I read texts again and again in different ways to master them; I don't simply suck up the words and understand them perfectly the first time through. Let's make the reading process explicit. Teachers can advise students to visualise the text and ask questions about it, but how exactly do students apply this advice and for what outcome? If we want students to visualise then we need to manoeuvre them towards the important things to imagine, and we do this by guiding their questioning through cold reading strategies.

Cold reading turns the intimidating and potentially overwhelming experience of grappling with an unknown text into a predictable and controllable experience. It draws attention to how reading strategies must develop along the reading continuum in order to build on previous ideas, and that re-reading by itself is not an effective method.

Students who can cold read well do not have to make a special study of set texts in depth to think and write intelligently about them. As we know any extract can crop up in the exam, it's unrealistic to expect students to have hot read every line. Cold reading means we are able to teach certain parts of the set texts and catch students up more quickly. Moreover, the skill transfers to the Language papers (and indeed to any exam that requires the processing of text).

It's also a type of formative assessment, where you can check for understanding or misconceptions before more inferential readings happen. Sometimes, the most impressive inference is merely the wrong end of the stick in disguise! As English teachers, it's too easy to be seduced by an 'original' response.

---

6. Labov, W. and Waletzky, J. 'Narrative Analysis: Oral Versions of Personal Experience', *Journal of Narrative and Life History*, 7, 3–38.

Additionally, cold reading is a 'pre' and 'during' reading strategy that allows students to take a metacognitive approach to the text.[7] Mccrea's report asserts that 'what we know determines what we can learn'. [8]This means we learn if we have some existing framework of a subject. Essentially, text is the problem that we'll equip our students to solve – and not just the set texts, but any text. We'll do this by giving them a basic toolkit or frame of reference first, through making informed predictions about texts in general.

COLD READING: HOW?

It can help if you model cold reading with texts that are genuinely new to you, but you can also consciously 'put your cold reading hat on' with a text you already know to illustrate that **reading is a process of deliberate choices**. If you narrate not only your understanding but your *methods* of understanding as you read for the first time, you show that it is a tentative and cumulative process; you show that you will change your method later on; and you show that you can change your inferences too.

Let's see how this could be done with William Blake's 'A Poison Tree':[9]

I was angry with my friend
I told my wrath, my wrath did end.
I was angry with my foe:
I told it not, my wrath did grow.

And I water'd it in fears,
Night and morning with my tears;
And I sunned it with smiles,
And with soft deceitful wiles.

And it grew both day and night,
Till it bore an apple bright;

---

7. Cold reading can be a pre-reading strategy if we ask students to recount the general ingredients of a text.
8. Mccrea, P. (2019) *Learning: What Is It and How Might We Catalyse It?* Ambition Institute.
9. Blake, W. (2019) *Songs of Innocence and Experience.* London: Macmillan

And my foe beheld it shine,
And he knew that it was mine,

And into my garden stole
When the night had veil'd the pole:
In the morning glad I see
My foe outstretch'd beneath the tree.

Although it can seem obvious to us, students (especially under exam pressure) often forget to look at the title. Another curious thing I noticed when watching mock exams was students fixating on the centre of the extract. To help them relax, I recommend beginning with a skim read. This is simply to get their eyes moving in the right way and to show that the text is mostly made of language they can understand. It's a bit like limbering up before sport. It also helps us to disengage from anything else that has been holding our attention. Maryanne Wolf explains the neurological changes as we read in *Reader, Come Home* and says it begins with moving on from what we were previously attending to.[10] Make sure students know that they have to make a 'switch' to reading mode. Wolf also describes how the eyes move differently when taking in digital text, which may account for my observation in the mock exams. Therefore, it's beneficial for students to witness the movement of my eyes too.

Then my script when first encountering the extract might go something like this:

'I'm going to read the extract for the first time and this is probably going to make me feel a little nervous. But I know from my reading continuum that my first reads will be about me getting an idea or two about the poem that could change when I look closer. This is fine. The first impression the poem gives me isn't the only impression the poet wants to give. I also know that my cold reading training means I have special things to look out for, like who or what might be in conflict and if any of the objects in the poem might stand for other things.

I'll give the poem a skim first. (It helps if you can mime this, exaggerating the action a little. Demonstrate that skim reading moves down the page

---

10. Wolf, M. (2018) *Reader, Come Home*. New York: Harper Collins.

whereas closer reading moves across it.) *I won't understand much at this point but this action reassures me that I will. I recognise most of the words. Already, 'angry' has stuck with me and I'm thinking this poem will have much pathos. I'm going to write that at the top of the extract.*

Now, I'll look at the title – 'A Poison Tree'. This fits my initial inkling and I'm wondering what a poison tree might do and how it might grow. Will the poet describe an actual tree or will this be a symbol for other ideas? A method I'm using here is checking if the image is literal or metaphorical. I know texts use lots of symbols, so what might poison symbolise? Poison makes me think of harm and pollution, whereas tree is normally emblematic of rebirth. It's likely then that the poem will discuss these themes in some way. I'll jot those themes down.

I'm going to read the poem through now as a whole and just see what I feel. If a word is unfamiliar, it could be in the glossary at the bottom. However, if I'm unsure of any unexplained words, I'm not going to fixate on them. I'll focus on the language that stands out to me. I can sense the rage growing in the poem as I've noticed that angry and anger reappear, but the death at the end of the poem has satisfied my curiosity about the tree itself. I wondered what it would do. I find the image of the person lying beneath the tree disturbing and I think the poison tree is sinister.

I'm not as 'cold' on the poem now. At this stage I'll gather my thoughts: anger – harm – danger – shock. I've answered what the poem is about in some way, but I think I need to work out who's experiencing this and why, so I'm going to orientate or position myself more in the poem. I'm going to re-read stanza by stanza. It helps me if I ask three questions about each stanza:

1. *What happens?*

2. *What conflicts or problems does/can this cause?*

3. *What seems to be changing or staying the same?*

I'm going to note down my answers on the poem itself.

1. *What: In the first stanza, we have the speaker, a friend and a foe. We have the speaker angry with his friend and foe.*

2. *Conflicts: The speaker is unable to tell his foe of his anger so it grows.*

3. *Changes: The speaker's anger towards the foe is stronger.*

At this point I look back at my orientation notes and think, how does this information support the title? I can see that that the growing anger is like a poison tree, so this is a metaphor for the speaker's wrath. The anger is feeding the tree. This is surprising me because we often speak of things that grow in optimistic terms. The poet seems to be teaching me that we can nurture the wrong things, perhaps. A method we're using here is thinking of this poem as a lesson. What is it the poet wants to teach me? Also, I feel the speaker seems quite uncaring about his foe's feelings.

I'll move to the next stanza. My ideas might change here. This is good – the poet has carried the poem on so he wants my thoughts to develop. Immediately, my feelings are changing. The speaker shows their fear. I'm wondering what harm the foe has done. Should I have been more sympathetic towards the speaker? Now I know the actions of the poem in some detail, or the 'what' questions, I'm going to move further into closer reading. This might mean that I begin to think about individual lexis. Which words influence my feelings towards the speaker? I'm curious that the speaker smiles. How is the anger enjoyable? I'm using questioning as a method to deepen my ideas. And I can see that the smiles are linked to the sun; nature is appearing dangerous here. The poet might be teaching us that human nature is cruel. I'm beginning to think of this poem as an allegory on revenge.

This might seem ridiculously long and even patronising. I'm aware that students have limited time in the exam but they will get quicker at the process. This is the slow-motion version and I model this for students of all abilities. I do move faster and omit parts at times, but I always demonstrate to all students that reading is a process of deliberate choices and methods.

Often, the seemingly more able students can make silly mistakes because they don't believe that the earlier part of the reading continuum is needed. Students have also said things along the lines of 'Of course you get it, you're an English teacher!' English can be one of those subjects where teachers say a lot, but show little. A PE teacher would never just say 'Score more goals!' but would demonstrate tackling, ball control, etc. Sometimes, English teachers can be guilty of giving instructions like 'Please read the extract. What do you find out about Rochester? Now answer: How is Rochester presented', without directing students in how to do this skilfully.

I found that reading a text in this painstaking way was especially successful when teaching remotely during lockdown. I'd realised that many of my students were skim reading the poems and then rushing on to write their analyses. This wasn't surprising as I'd spent lots of time demonstrating how to craft an essay but little on how to garner the content of the essay. Therefore, we spent a week modelling reading to each other. I began in the way I've outlined above and I also used a random novel extract I'd never seen before to make me more aware of the strategies I was applying and to increase students' confidence. If I stumbled on a word, was uncertain or needed time to think, it showed students that this is natural as we move along the continuum.

The next time, I posed the reading more as a problem. I.e. I've got to read something I've never read before in front of you. I need to explain some ideas in the text. I feel a bit nervous about this. How do I solve my problem? I gathered together students' advice and then modelled the process again before asking them to model with me. Students can then practise the process independently. In this way, the reading process becomes part of the 'I do, we do, you do' cycle that many teachers use (although this approach doesn't seem to be used that often for the pure act of reading). It begins with the teacher demonstrating or modelling, then students start contributing to this, gradually taking more control and directing the teacher. Eventually students are given time to practise with less support.

The key to this process is to use shorter extracts to begin with. I find if we begin with extracts that match the length of the exam ones, students are overfaced and want to 'get through' the text rather than taking their time to apply the strategies.

It's also effective to gather students together after their first couple of reads to exchange ideas. I ask students where they are on the reading continuum now they've been given a different interpretation. Some say they're on a preliminary reading because it's a new idea they're focusing on; others explain that it's analytical reading because they're questioning a version of the text. Both answers are valid but it demonstrates that the reading process is never over.

Some students can be reluctant to write down their ideas as they feel they're not right. I don't approve of the 'whatever you think the poem's about is okay, it's your interpretation' school of thought because this flies in the face of writing being a conscious act of construction. But students do analyse better when they feel their first ideas can be tentative and exploratory.

LABOV'S NARRATIVE MODEL

As mentioned earlier, an effective framework to note initial impressions is Labov's narrative model. The framework asks readers to orientate themselves in a text and move through the conflicts towards a resolution; it also provides questions for students to ask as they read. It's a faster version of the script above. I believe that all students should explore the reading process slowly and in as much detail as possible at least once a term, but this framework can be used when students are familiar with the idea of the continuum. Labov's narrative model is not only speedier, but also reflects the way stories are spoken and so links to students' innate ability to narrate. This framework allows you to illustrate or check for basic comprehension, but also builds towards evaluation; in fact, this mirrors the ascendency of skills on the Language papers.

I've demonstrated the model below. This is a genuine response from a group of students who found reading difficult. We looked at an unseen text, Neil Gaiman's 'Don't Ask Jack', in a remote lesson. This is how students filled in the grid.

Orientation	Jack
Who?	A toy
What?	Past
When?	The nursery
Where?	Children
POINT: The writer uses the symbol of… to…	Old-fashioned
	Wealthy
Complicating action (conflict)	The children don't play with the toy.
What?	It's an antique – doesn't work as well.
EXPLANATION: This is further supported by…	The children don't like the toy.
	Abandoned toy.
	Jack is frightening.
	The toy is broken.
	They leave the house and forget about it.
	Haunted by the box.
	WW1.
	Bad memories in the house.
	Try to burn it down.
Resolution	Supernatural force in the box.
Finally	The children's belief could be the problem.
Coda	
ANALYSIS: This is to make us aware that… as evidenced by the use of…	
Evaluation	Personal experience – shared.
Why?	Sympathy for children.
So what?	Fear of the unknown.
RESPONSE: This has the effect of…	How to manage fear.
	What we should really be scared of.
Abstract	An antique toy that frightens children.
What's it about?	The children overstate the importance of the toy.
RESPONSE: Moreover, there is an awareness of…	Childhood fears.
	The supernatural is manipulative – it has a psychological effect.

I begin by explaining a little about the framework itself. Labov collected lots of spoken stories and identified the patterns that narratives contain. This helps us to predict what we'll find in all narratives. It's like a compass that orients us in the text, and once we're oriented securely, we can move around the text and think more deeply about it. We won't get 'lost' because we've kept a basic map.

With more skilful readers, we'll often read the text in its entirety first. I've noticed that less confident readers need to keep track more, so those groups fill in as we go along. This means they aren't worrying about the previous paragraph when they're trying to comprehend the next one. Cognitive load theory tells us that the working memory can be overwhelmed when reading, preventing thorough comprehension of the text as a whole.[11] Labov's model can function as a schema (a representation of how the brain organises information) so that students can focus on using, not retaining, this information to further understand the text.

My classes usually read the opening paragraph or two and fill in the first box. The answers are not definite so if new information is revealed we can alter our thoughts. It's helpful to split the text into opening, middle and closing sections and pause to fill in the grid at each juncture, but as I've said, we can move backwards and forwards. The conflict box is likely to be returned to often, for example.

When students become proficient, they can swap grids with each other and compare ideas. I once gave a class a range of extracts from different parts of Macbeth. Students had to work out which scene their partner had tracked trough the model. This might seem obvious, and indeed students are mostly able to say, 'It's the scene where *Macbeth* hallucinates the dagger'. But what makes this valuable is the debate raised by the conflict, resolution and evaluation boxes in particular. One student couldn't reconcile the dagger scene with his partner's evaluation that the scene had been included to show Macbeth wasn't in control of his actions. The first student was convinced that it was precisely to show him being resolute. Yet both students agreed it was important that Macbeth was

---

11. Sweller, J., Ayres, P. and Kalugua, S. (2011) *Cognitive Load Theory*. Sydney: Springer.

alone because it meant he was truly being himself. I found it fascinating how they disagreed though about which 'true' self was being revealed. Not only do the grids provoke discussion, they make useful summaries of chapters and revision sources too.

Once students have completed the grid, they can explore the ideas in an analytical essay. I usually ask students to read over their models and then to find quotations to support the most interesting ideas. This means students respond to the text first before seizing on random quotes. For 'Don't Ask Jack', I posed the question: How does Gaiman present the theme of fear? Students used their grids to help them construct their thesis statement (the central idea their essay would explore). For example: *Fear can be used to manipulate others. Both young and old appear controlled by fear in the text.*

They then looked at the 'orientation' information and used this as a symbol of fear. For example: *The nursery should be a safe space but shows us that terror can strike anywhere.* Even basic information can be transformed into an insightful comment in this way. Students can create points from the orienting information such as: *The writer uses the nursery as symbol of false security.*

The most fertile quotations are often to be found in the 'complicating action' box, whereas most of the analytical comments are in the 'evaluation' box. In the model above, I also inserted some sentence starters to indicate how students are to use the model as a map to direct their analysis. The framework also supports when they 'speak' an essay too; not all extended answers have to be written. Furthermore, I've used students' frameworks and then modelled an extended response from them as well.

The grid's efficacy is increased when students link parts of the model to the reading continuum. For example, when students are evaluating, I ask: Where are we on the continuum? What strategies do we have to help us evaluate?

Don't think the model can't be used for higher-order questions too: simply asking where a scene in a play happens can provoke deeper analysis. My class spent a long time exploring the significance of the witches' cave in *Macbeth*. Inferences ranged from socioeconomic symbolism of disenfranchised women to the effects of eschatological imagery! Don't feel that you're wasting time by breaking texts and extracts down through Labov's model. You simply don't have time to excavate and quash misconceptions later and to repair the damage done. Happily, the framework can be used for planning writing tasks and even peer assessment when students read each other's texts. In terms of reading anything, they now have a basic map that can direct the way towards critical analysis.

FOLLOW MY LEADER

As students' cold reading skills develop, you can move on to the 'Follow my leader' strategy. This is a lighter version of Labov's model, more suited to exam extracts, but it still links to the idea that all texts contain conflict, whether micro or macro, thereby aiding students to uncover the text's central concerns. These conflicts or problems can be macro, like Eva's struggle against the class system in *An Inspector Calls*, but they can also be micro, as in Sheila's teasing of her father about the port. Literature is defined by having a central conflict at its heart and by the idea that a narrative must include some element of change because of this conflict. The conflict or change can seem slight, as in Joyce's short stories where the character realises (often privately) something about themselves, or it can be more transformative, as in the fall of Shakespeare's tragic heroes, but all texts contain problems and developments.

If we're looking at an exam extract, I'll ask students to take a glance at the exam question first but not to be constrained by this when reading the extract for the first time. The writer of the text is in charge of directing their responses, not the writer of the exam question. In 'Follow my leader', students move through the text, stopping at moments of conflict and then places of change, to consider their impressions and to note significant information.

This technique lets them know that they are in a sense being manipulated by the writer. The writer focuses our attention on specific details to influence our view. For example, let's use this strategy on an extract from

Lord of the Flies.[12] I've kept it short to illustrate the process more clearly. Students can apply it to individual paragraphs/stanzas, but it works well for a general overview of the text that will then allow them to move along the reading continuum to close reads.

Long before Ralph and Piggy came up with Jack's lot they could hear the party. There was a stretch of grass in a place where the palms left a wide band of turf between the forest and the shore. Just one step down from the edge of the turf was the white, blown sand of above high water, warm, dry, trodden. Below that again was a rock that stretched away toward the lagoon. Beyond was a short stretch of sand and then the edge of the water. A fire burned on the rock and fat dripped from the roasting pig meat into the invisible flames. All the boys of the island, except Piggy, Ralph, Simon, and the two tending the pig, were grouped on the turf. They were laughing, singing, lying, squatting, or standing on the grass, holding food in their hands. But to judge by the greasy faces, the meat eating was almost done; and some held coconut shells in their hands and were drinking from them. Before the party had started, a great log had been dragged into the centre of the lawn and Jack, painted and garlanded, sat there like an idol. There were piles of meat on green leaves near him and fruit and coconut shells full of drink.

> **What:** Piggy, Ralph and Simon can see the other boys having a kind of party.
>
> **Conflict:** The three boys are not involved. The other boys have had meat too, which is unfair. The three boys are against the others but will also probably be conflicted by their appetites.
>
> **Changes:** By the end, the three boys are not the only ones removed. Jack is also apart but this seems to be as if he's being worshipped and given offerings.

This is a very effective way for a student to keep track of their thoughts and for light annotation of the extract. I advise most students to use this as their first reading strategy when faced with an exam extract, after they've taken a calming skim of it. It also means that students don't begin by highlighting potentially useless chunks and trying to zoom in on a word before comprehending it in its wider context.

One of my proudest moments as a teacher was witnessing a class reading sample exam extracts having really struggled in the past. They ignored

---

12. Golding, W. (1997) *Lord of the Flies.* London: Faber and Faber.

the highlighters, had their pens ready, and actually wrote *notes*. I trained them by not only marking their responses to an exam-style question, but also 'marking' their annotation of the extract. Had they followed the advice? Were their notes organised? Had they taken any words out of context? Had they written the strategies at the top of the extract?

This approach ensures that students' first readings are rigorous and so lessens the danger of vague interpretations later on. It also means that students can better position the extract in relation to the whole text. For example, they can look at their 'Follow my leader' notes and consider: Where else in the text are the boys splitting into different factions? What are the consequences of this later on?

WHO VS WHO?

'Follow my leader' can lead to 'Who vs who?', which builds on the theme of conflict and develops students' understanding that all texts include problems, whilst steering them towards the most revealing ones. Cold reading is teaching students that texts will include similar ingredients, so they should be primed to spot conflict. Here students identify the specific types of conflict that are occurring in a text. This goes back to Aristotle's view that drama should contain a single unifying conflict. Various types of conflict have been identified but a useful starting point is this short list:

- Person vs person
- Person vs nature
- Person vs society
- Person vs themselves

In the *Lord of the Flies* extract above, we have the boys versus each other, versus nature, versus themselves and versus the newly emerging hierarchy. Not all of these will be relevant for the question that students have to answer, but they give a fuller picture of the extract. Students sometimes complain that 'there's nothing in the extract', but this example illustrates that a very small sample of text has a number of micro-conflicts.

Macro-conflicts help us to comprehend the text in general. Micro-conflicts are a great way to look deeper at a character's role and to understand their motivations and actions, and will move us closer to 'hot' reading (i.e. analysing). For example, once we know that Juliet is against her parents, we have to ask why Shakespeare has shown us this. Is it to demonstrate her folly of her parents' folly? What if we see her parents as a symbol of authority in general? What is Juliet 'against' now?

This prepares students for questions about the characters but also about themes. If we're asked 'How does Shakespeare present rebellion in *Romeo and Juliet*?', we can see it's really a question about characters because characters act out the theme and will be in conflict with it in some way. Equally, if we're asked 'How does Shakespeare present Juliet?', we know it's a theme question because we have to look at who and what she is opposed to/in conflict with. All literature questions are really asking what the conflict in the text is. Why is this conflict important? What does the writer want us to think about this conflict?

For those students who find it difficult to make inferences under pressure, or who can be overwhelmed by the text, we can help by teaching some general (but not too general) inferences attached to these conflicts.

For example, in *An Inspector Calls*, Birling is against:

Persons:
- Eva and therefore his workers: Birling sees his staff as a tool of commerce and wealth, not as real people. Priestley wants us to understand how business exploits its workers and sees them as part of a machine.
- Sheila: Birling is patronising towards his daughter, disregarding her views. Priestley seems to be drawing our attention to how women are silenced by the patriarchy.

Self:
- Birling has to fight his own panic and terror at the possibility of losing his status. This frightens him more than the cruelty inflicted on Eva, so Priestley illustrates that Birling's morality is skewed. We might also wonder how Birling can be a powerful patriarch when he finds it difficult to control his own fears.

ARCHETYPE GUESS WHO

Another cold reading strategy is to match archetypes to characters in the text. Archetypes symbolise some basic concepts, so students can anticipate the values that will likely recur. The strategy 'Archetype guess who' helps students to categorise characters and see them more as constructs than as actual people. This helps with comments like 'Why doesn't Eva just...?', 'If I was Desdemona, I'd lamp him', etc.

Jung categorised the personality into sub-groups or archetypes. Although potentially limitless in number, there are several archetypes that are recurrent in literature. These can be literal but are more likely to play a symbolic role in the text. They don't have to be obvious interpretations, as the table below makes clear.

Archetype	General themes inherent in the archetype	Example	Inferences
The parent (guardian, creator)	Power, legacy, control, experience, wisdom	Lady Macbeth functions as scolding parent, disappointed by her 'child', the infantilised Macbeth.	Proud, protective, possessive, domineering, disappointed
The child (ingénue)	Innocence, exploitation, power, growing up	King Duncan's naivety is almost childlike; the unthinking optimism of the castle's 'pleasant air'.	Naive, untainted, pliable, innocent, vulnerable
The devil (rebel, tempter, subconscious)	Subversion, protest, power, resistance	The witches can be seen as devils as they tempt Macbeth whilst they rebel against dominant ideology.	Radical, challenging, shocking, alternative
The sage (wiseman, teacher, mentor, role model)	Wisdom, experience, education, nurture	The porter reveals the failures of sex could be at the root of Macbeth's inadequacy.	Revelatory, mouthpiece, possibly authorial voice
The trickster	Experience, trust, deceit, power, disappointment	The witches fit this again, but possibly Lady Macbeth and even Macbeth himself in the (feigned?) aporia in the dagger soliloquy.	Manipulative, exploitative, malignant, destructive
The hero	Pride, power, achievement, adversity	Macduff restores order.	Conservative, restorative, benevolent, honourable

When students are given an extract from a set text, this method can help them orient it. For instance, if the extract is from a scene with the witches, Macbeth is more of an ingénue here, meaning we can have a more sympathetic response. We can then comment on how this is challenged when Macbeth murders another ingénue, Duncan, almost making the betrayal of his kinsman even worse.

I introduce the archetypes to students first and ask them how they might describe each one, and what role they might play in society and in literature. Once they've got the idea of the archetypes, they sort characters into the categories, justifying their choices. This can be an interesting physical task too. Students can create different postures for each archetype, such as crouching as the ingénue or hiding their faces as the trickster. As we read a text, I ask students to assume the pose of the archetype they think the character is inhabiting.

THE FOUR HUMOURS

The approach above can be developed by combining it with some knowledge of the four humours.

The four humours (said to have originated with Hippocrates) is a way of characterising personality that has influenced many writers, but is particularly evident in Shakespeare. The humours are bodily fluids linked to personality traits, and it was believed that people's characters were dictated by having more of one fluid than another.

- Blood = sanguine (cheerful)
- Black bile = melancholic (miserable)
- Yellow bile = choleric (angry)
- Phlegm = phlegmatic (calm)

We can see that Macbeth's character is mostly choleric and melancholic, but Lady Macbeth can manage to be sanguine! This can help students to visualise characters more easily, make predictions and even inform their own creative writing, whilst providing some lower-frequency lexis. When students cold read and much of their attention is focused on decoding, it can mean their explanations and responses are expressed rather simplistically. The four humours splits characters into happy, sad etc. but uses sophisticated language to do this. Students will read and note the emotions of characters but will use the humours framework to describe them more aptly and to help flesh out inferences. Thinking of melancholia in terms of black bile gets them thinking about its sickly qualities – that it's like a disease that can't be shaken off, that it makes the character seem almost faded. They begin to explore what the emotion is like and the themes it links to rather than just identifying it in the text.

The humours are associated with times of the year too. I introduce the theory of the four humours by asking students which season they feel best describes each one. They explain why, considering the connotations and symbolism of the season. I wonder if another season might be more fitting when their circumstances change. I say, would you still be this season the night before an exam? After the birth of your first child? This begins to illustrate that the characters in texts will develop. I then repeat this with characters from a text before revealing which humour the students and the characters would be defined by.

- Blood = spring

- Black bile = autumn

- Yellow bile = summer

- Phlegm = winter

This strategy allows students to predict, describe and evaluate perspectives, but also helps when they come to create their own characters. The categorisation could be applied to atmosphere and tone and changes in structure. In *A Christmas Carol*, each stave can be characterised by a humour. Stave One is choleric; Stave Two is melancholic and sanguine, etc. Students can discuss why the writer wants to evoke these atmospheres. It can make students respond more imaginatively to questions about setting too. (If Thornfield Hall had a humour, what would it be?)

I also find it interesting that summer is linked to what might be perceived as a less desirable humour (choleric). This allows students to explore subversion as flourishing and beneficial. When I asked my students why Macbeth might be associated with summer, they were able to explain that he is a radical, fighting back against a limiting and austere regime. This means students begin to think of alternative interpretations.

The table below aids students in their general understanding of the roles characters have in texts and how they contribute to the main themes. If we say that Ralph in Lord of the Flies is an initially sanguine character, students can predict that he is likely to be popular but that his self-assurance is going to be challenged. The humours take us back again to the dominant theme of conflict because we can predict that a character's humour will be tested, developed, subverted or transformed in some way. We can then begin to question why, for example, Golding wants us to see Ralph's confidence and self-assurance taking a bashing. What does this tell us about the human experience in general?

Humour	Connected lexis	Season	Element	Likely themes
Sanguine (blood)	Optimistic Confidence Energetic Hedonistic Dionysian Satisfiedy	Spring	Air	Identity Morality Redemption Rebirth Glory Survival Order
Choleric (yellow bile)	Angry Irascible Resentful Frustrated Resistant Rebellious Dystopian Turbulent Disenfranchised	Summer	Fire	Identity Rebellion Destruction Creation Adversity Power Survival Disorder
Melancholic (black bile)	Pessimistic Lugubrious Dispirited Disappointed Dystopian	Autumn	Earth	Identity Death Obscurity Isolation Corruption Disorder
Phlegmatic (phlegm)	Placid Apollonian Pragmatic Practical Dispassionate Conservative Traditional Franchised	Winter	Water	Identity Order Reason Apathy

The cold reading strategies above show students that all texts will:

1. Give information (who, what, where) that will orientate us in the text

2. Contain conflicts and problems

3. Attempt to influence our opinion and response on these problems

4. Contain some element of change

5. Explore the common roles people play in society

6. Elucidate the conflicts that arise from these roles

Whether or not students have already read the extract that appears in the exam will be less important when they understand that the above ingredients are constants (a code) that lead us to the closer reads on the reading continuum.

Strategy: Cold reading	
Good for...	**Sub-strategies**
• **First and second reads.**	• Labov's narrative model
• Comprehension.	• Model your first read
• Reading the exam extract in context.	• Follow my leader
• Preparing for unseen texts.	• Who vs who?
• Reading each other's texts.	• Archetype guess who
• Creating success criteria for writing tasks.	• The four humours

HOT READING: WHAT?

Hot reading means students have already read the text a few times and have a solid comprehension, or have done some deliberate study of the text previously. Hot reading encourages students to think more about the text as a whole and how their inferences have developed throughout. It allows for deeper, less generic ideas so that we move into the second half of the reading continuum.

Whilst cold reading mostly supports comprehension, hot reading is more analytical, but still relies on a basic initial understanding.

We could call hot reading close reading, yet it is still informed by wider textual knowledge outside of a specific work. That is, we'll return to the common codes that cold reading has identified.

HOT READING: WHY?

Having different strategies on the reading continuum lets students see the reading process and gives them autonomy in choosing the strategy they need to best comprehend the text.

Hot reading is also a clear segue into closer reading, which means accessing different skills. It is a plain signal to 'shift gear' and prevent the complaints of 'I've already read it!' Just as we'd plan, draft and edit when writing, this reading process shows we refine our comprehension in distinct stages. We can change our mind and our response; reading is fluid.

You can't leap ahead to hot reading. I recall skipping the first stages of cold reading and blithely ploughing ahead with 'The Charge of the Light Brigade' because of time pressures. When we returned to the poem two weeks later, horrifying misconceptions ambushed me and the students wallowed in a valley of misinformation. Because I hadn't asked the basic what/where/when questions, many students hadn't visualised the battle and some even got it mixed up with the fire brigade!

Hot reading transforms our students into literary scholars. They must be aware of the difference between reading for understanding and then reading to discover how this understanding has been transmitted to the reader. That is, once students have a concept of the text, they need to explain how the writer conveyed this concept to them. Students do not need to have looked at every word of every set text in order to comment meaningfully because cold reading will have uncovered the concepts, and hot reading will equip them to comment on how these concepts are constructed in the text.

HOT READING: HOW?

Crucially, hot reading can only build on secure cold reading. If students haven't understood the text, remain at a cold (or at least lukewarm) level until you can safely move on. This must be established first.

Any strategy that builds on an initial understanding can be a hot reading strategy (although some work better in exam conditions). Simply put, cold reading is about the 'what' questions, whilst hot reading moves to the 'how' and 'why'.

Students need to know that the readings the text allows are never over (see the reading continuum). But they also need to recognise that they can over-analyse. A general rule is: have students found three important ideas that will link to the question? If they have, they don't need to apply more strategies. As the school year progresses, I also allow students to decide which methods help them best. It's effective to have discussions with students about this and to type up their individual strategy menus.

POWER GAMES

We return to the idea of conflict when we first begin to hot read. 'Power games' builds on from 'Who vs who?' and can eventually be linked to the ideology explored in the text. Power is more of a hot rather than cold technique because it can be more subtle.

With this strategy I ask students to note down the characters in the text. We consider how powerful they've been overall in the text and give them a mark out of ten. For example, I might feel that Jo (*A Taste of Honey*)[13] is 5/10 because she asserts herself but allows her will to be influenced by others. I might say Geof is 3/10 because he's relying on Jo to provide him with a 'normal life'. What about the unborn child? Let's consider how much power it has. I'll say 7/10 whilst its unborn as the baby is limiting Jo's freedom and making Geof ripe for exploitation.

Then we read the text, noting where this power increases or decreases for the characters. What does this tell us about them at that moment? How will this increase/decrease in power influence what is to come? Who do we think should have the most power? Why might this be/not be the case?

---

13. Delaney, S. (2008) *A Taste of Honey*. London: Methuen Drama.

To illustrate the power games method, I'm going to talk through Act Two, Scene One from *A Taste of Honey*, where Jo is restless and Geof is attempting to calm her.

Initially, Jo is 4/10 – Jo is feeling trapped by her body and her cramped home.

However, Geof (5/10) seems more powerful because he's ordering Jo to take it easy.

Jo then criticises their home.

Jo = 3/10 Her power seems to be decreasing as she realises she'd still be trapped by her situation if she left the flat.

Geof = 5/10 Geof is becoming more of an advocate for other 'stuck' people as he defends their neighbours.

Jo = 5/10 – Jo comments on children in her community. Judging others seems to increase her sense of self-worth, especially as she disparages another mother.

Geof = 6/10 – Geof, tactfully, tries to change the subject. He seems aware that Jo could really be admonishing herself. He could make more of this but uses his power here to soothe Jo. We can see Geof's compassion is stronger than his will to dominate. He employs power to nurture, not to attack.

However, as Jo becomes more irritable, Geof's power diminishes.

Geof = 4/10 – Geof's control falters. Is he concerned that Jo will upset herself? Is he thinking that a criticism of her maternal skills might lead to a criticism of him as 'father'?

The baby kicks Jo and now seems to have agency. 7/10 for the baby because it's finally halted the growing tension. Does this show that the baby will be a transformative force? Will the baby calm Jo?

Geof puts his head to Jo's stomach.

Geof = 2/10. He appears to be bowing to the baby's power.

Jo picks up Geof's dress-making, addresses the baby and refers to Geof as 'big sister.'

Jo = 6/10 She reasserts her power by feminising Geof and reminding him of his lesser role in their relationship.

It shows it's alive anyway. Come on, baby, let's see what big sister's making for us. (*6/10 – Jo reasserts her power by feminising Geof and reminding him of his lesser role in their relationship.*)

GEOF

Put it down.

JO

What a pretty little dress.

I'd then ask who has the ultimate power in the scene. The baby hints at the changes to come for Jo, and her taunting of Geof at the scene's close strips him of any real power. The dominant power could be the image of a 'normal' family. Jo and Geof might be less powerful because they don't fit this.

When students are annotating extracts in the exam, they could judge power in the opening, middle and end of an extract to make the process more rapid.

The person or thing with power is the crux of the text: no matter what students are asked to analyse, it will link to this central tension. We can also see that shifts and developments in power are a structural technique as well. The use of archetypes when cold reading (see page 37) means that characters can be defined in terms of a power hierarchy, giving a solid basis for students' answers.

For instance, students need to know that Geof is gay to really understand the power shift at the scene's close, so power fits hot reading more, but our cold reading knowledge of the parent archetype would mean we could decode Geof as a type of parent figure for Jo. We can detect the irony in the pregnant character falling into the role of ingénue, so we would perceive vulnerability, suggesting that Geof would be the most powerful. We could consider the traditions of the patriarchy here. However, knowing about the devil archetype illustrates Jo's rebellion. Is Delaney hinting at how women are questioning their societal roles? We might match her to the trickster too as she allows Geof into her world before insulting him. Even if we didn't know about Geof's sexuality, the closing lines would illuminate Jo grasping back her power and her rejection of Geof as a parent figure. In a broader sense, this scene seems to depict how 'children' will inevitably eschew parental force. We can see here that archetypes allow us to explicate the power shifts in more detail and to link them to broader themes.

ALL IS ALLEGORY

When students' inferences are cursory or obvious, an allegorical approach has borne much fruit in my lessons. Many teachers seem to shy away from teaching this to LPA students, but how will they ever understand that the writer makes conscious decisions about the language without it? We know allegorical awareness is essential for *Lord of the Flies* and *A Christmas Carol*, but with this approach, I have students pretend that every text is an allegory. This means they have to consider the implicit ideas more deeply, sharpening their inferences. They don't need to explicitly mention these ideas in their answers (though symbolism is a very handy technical term); only to generate them. It means that students look for deeper messages and see the characters and events as symbols, not just as reportage. For me this has proven to be one of the quickest fixes for students of all abilities.

Make sure students have a sound literal meaning first by employing 'Follow my leader' (page 33) or Labov's narrative model (page 29). Once the literal message is plain, we can explore the hidden layers of meaning. This works well in poetry where every line is like a slice of layered cake. I ask students to read the text, finding at least one key object in each paragraph/stanza. For example, if I applied this to Sylvia Plath's 'Morning Song', I might say the gold watch is the key object in the opening stanza. I need to be careful not to just seize on this but to enquire what it is doing and how it's described. The baby is as active and as valuable as a watch, maybe. What message is coming through? I think the message is: the mother's time with the child is too short.

Now, what is the key symbol in the second stanza? Does this symbol support or subvert the initial message? The next symbol is 'statue'. This seems to contradict the vitality of the ticking watch. A statue is still. Stillness could symbolise the mother's constant love for the child. The message might be that time will change the child but not the mother's love. Then I'll move into the third stanza. I'm drawn to the 'mirror' that shows the bond between mother and baby, but also shows a grown woman. The speaker has changed as the child must. At this point, as I'm halfway through the poem, I'll reconsider the first symbol. I thought the watch stood for the baby's potential but the symbol also applies to how the mother is changed by time. It's apparent how layer after layer of meaning is revealed in this way. By the poem's close, I would ask students to find a superordinate message in the poem and at least two subordinate ones. That is, what is the main message, and what other messages slip through? Do they confirm or deny the overarching message?

TEXT AS TEACHER

Students use hot reading to identify the themes in the text and to identify the overarching messages. They should already be aware that texts are the best teachers in the world and they can begin to explore this didacticism explicitly. Quite simply, what is the text hoping to teach us? *How* does it teach us? It's a great way to display the artifice of texts; ask students to imagine that the writer has to keep a class of students entertained but must also teach them something new. How do they keep our attention? How do they ensure we learn? And what do they do with 'naughty' readers? Are there any harder lessons in the text?

This works particularly well with *A Christmas Carol* as each stave can be seen as a lesson. If we examine the first stave, what are we being taught when Scrooge refuses to give to the charity collectors? We're entertained by the rudeness of Scrooge but the collectors' patient explanation informs us of others' needs, whilst also teaching us that Scrooge is cold. The silent but attendant Bob reminds us that our actions can be witnessed and judged. We also have to learn that some people really do lack sympathy.

The sentence starters 'The text teaches us…' and 'The reader learns…' really help students here who are strong verbally but struggle to get their ideas on paper. You can also ask students to reduce scenes/chapters etc. to a 'learning objective' to help them make texts more manageable. This can be a quick fix when students find it hard to begin. I might ask: if Carol Ann Duffy was teaching our lesson today, what would the learning objective be? I ask students to imagine the writer has set the text especially for their lesson. For instance, for 'War Photographer' my class suggested that the learning objective was that our society is desensitised to violence. Another student proposed the lesson was actually how pointless the role is, as a photographer can't compete with the experience.

The 'lessons' are inferences but it means students read with more purpose. They can then examine how the writer teaches us. That is, Duffy teaches the lesson of desensitisation through the regular shape of the poem – somehow the chaos and agony is accepted and compartmentalised by us. She also teaches us by modelling the process of developing a photograph – it's lonely, almost uncanny in a hellish red glow, so it exposes us to the worst of humanity.

THE TIME MACHINE

Another hot reading strategy is 'The time machine', where students identify the transhistorical themes in a text so they can create inferences. This doesn't mean that we spend a lot of time talking about the king or queen of the time but anticipate and explore the big ideas of all texts: class, race, gender. We can sum this up with the theme of identity. Ultimately, any text is concerned with the human experience. *Lord of the Rings* might present hobbits and wizards but it's still a story about the search for power; it's still about privilege; it's still about groups identifying themselves by difference or similarity to each other.

I introduce this idea by asking students what people's worries and problems are. Students suggest money, health, falling out, the environment, prejudice.

I ask if they think that current writers worry about these things too. We then explore what problems Victorians might have faced. Invariably, students create similar lists. It's fine if students understand that the Poor Law was changed so that support for the impoverished was reduced. It's much better if they feel the injustice of poverty in general and the inevitable consequences of it. If students are primed to look for attitudes to class in *A Christmas Carol* then they will perceive Scrooge's apathy and the long-term effects of this. Whether they really understand the isolated comment that 'The Treadmill and the Poor Law are in full vigour, then?' becomes much less important.

I often turn to Aristotle if I'm looking for inspiration for lessons or ways to explain theory. Another way I illustrate to students that texts are crammed with transhistorical ideas is through this quote from his *Politics*: 'One would have thought that it was even more necessary to limit population than property.' The class speculates on who said it and when. Rarely have students thought it was pre-twentieth century. Some link it to far-right ideas; others see it as an ecological comment. This shows how similar ideas might be perceived differently depending on the age, but ultimately testifies that the same ideas are constantly re-examined because they remain important.

We can also build on the 'Target practice' strategy here (page 14). The central theme in the target can be identity or split into the strands of race, class and gender. What does the writer argue about these themes? We can link to 'Text as teacher' too by asking, for example, what does the text want to teach us about race?

Students can discover comments on class by ranking the characters in the extract in order of importance. Does the most important deserve their importance? If not, why not? What does the writer want to show through this injustice?

I'll use an extract from Great Expectations[14] to talk through how I'd use transhistorical ideas as a hot reading strategy. Bear in mind that students should have already used a cold reading strategy to gain a basic knowledge of events. This is the episode where Pip meets Miss Havisham and we're going to use transhistorical themes to profile her.

---

14. Dickens, C. (1992) *Great Expectations*. Wordsworth Classics.

Whether I should have made out this object so soon, if there had been no fine lady sitting at it, I cannot say. In an arm-chair, with an elbow resting on the table and her head leaning on that hand, sat the strangest lady I have ever seen, or shall ever see.

She was dressed in rich materials – satins, and lace, and silks – all of white. Her shoes were white. And she had a long white veil dependent from her hair, and she had bridal flowers in her hair, but her hair was white.

When students close read, they look for clues about identity:

1. What is their gender? Students can anticipate the kind of limitations Miss Havisham is likely to have imposed on her as a woman. We would also look at how the writer lets us know her gender. Dickens doesn't just signify with pronouns but with the respectful 'lady.' She is likely to be less powerful than men in general but this title shows she's likely to have economic or cultural power over others. Will Pip feel intimidated by this?

2. Age? The white hair suggests her age. We know that some women feel they lose the little power they have with age.

3. Race? We can discuss the assumptions that are made here and the underrepresentation of non-white races. Dickens is not making an explicit comment on race but the absence of ethnic minorities is itself a comment on race. This might not link closely to the novel or be raised in exam questions, but it makes for a stimulating discussion.

4. Class? The listing of expensive material asserts her wealth and status.

5. Job/role? Unknown from this extract. Students can consider what they know about the context of the extract if it's a set text, but transhistoricism helps when students look at unseen passages too. We'll say this is a seen text, and we know that Miss Havisham has asked to be visited. In a strange way, she is almost a recipient of a charitable act. Whilst we know our expectations will be subverted, it seems as if she could also be the sage archetype. What might Pip learn from her?

6. Appearance? Her bridal clothes create a ghostly image as she is a remnant. She is dressed traditionally, perhaps hinting at her conservatism.

In this way, Miss Havisham's gender, class and age define her. Just by looking at a very small section of text with a transhistorical lens, we've uncovered some of her conflicts: this privileged and rich woman seems trapped in the past; money hasn't brought contentment; the limitations of status have frustrated the rich as much as the poor. We find that we can predict the behaviour of characters, events and perspectives because class, race and gender are often constraints that lead to conflict. Therefore, class, race and gender function as the underlying macro-theme of identify. Within these transhistorical ideas are the micro-themes of rebellion, tradition, progress, conformity, etc.

No matter what theme or character students are questioned on, they will be able to frame the answer in terms of what the characters or themes ultimately reveal about identity. For example, asking how Phil's presented in *DNA* is really asking about the themes of masculinity, power and youth. If the question asks how Dennis Kelly presents leadership, it's a question about Phil and so it's a question about masculinity, power and youth. Transhistorical readings simultaneously limit a text whilst making students focus on wider issues. We can illustrate this by using a *Romeo and Juliet* question too: 'How is Romeo presented?' is really asking about the themes of masculinity, power and youth.

THE RHETORICAL TRIANGLE

We can also help students identify the big ideas and the writer's attitude towards them through the rhetorical triangle.

Aristotle proposed three areas that writers must consider to be persuasive: ethos, logs and pathos. These are arranged in a triangle to show how it is desirable to balance them equally (Figure 4).

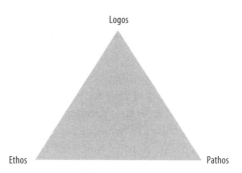

Figure 4: The rhetorical triangle

Aristotle was talking about persuasive speeches, but all writers, even writers of fiction and poetry, want to persuade us of something. This might be as simple as suspending our disbelief but is usually much greater. Fiction has to persuade us to care about pretend characters and events, but does so to persuade us of the importance of bigger ideas. Ultimately, writers of any text want us to think and care about what is written.

Teach students to look for an appeal to ethos, logos and pathos. Ethos means a sense of authority, credibility and/or personal experience; logos is about the use of reason and logic; pathos means engaging emotions. For me, this has proved really useful when students look at the non-fiction extracts for English Language. An effective strategy has been to build a paragraph around each of the ingredients when writing language analysis but it's also been a way into comparison. That is, students might explain how one writer appeals more strongly towards pathos, whilst one relies more heavily on logos. They might look at how a metaphor builds a sense of ethos in one text but is used emotively (pathos) in another.

We know that passages of Shakespeare can be intimidating for our students, especially if a lesser-known extract is presented in the exam. Rhetoric can help a student divide a text into more manageable chunks. Pathos can often be the easiest to find, so you can ask students to note down some emotions as they read. I then advise them to look for reasons why we should trust the speaker. Logos and ethos link together as logical explanations can make us trust a speaker. For ethos, I advise looking for anything about the speaker themselves, so things like inclusive address, anecdotes, etc. It can be helpful to look again for pathos as this can be subtler than a simple 'This means the speaker is happy/sad'.

Let's look at ethos, pathos and logos in the opening of the St Crispin's Day speech from Henry V. [15]

The fewer men, the greater share of honour. ◄———— **Logos:** fewer men = more glory

God's will! I pray thee, wish not one man more.

But if it be a sin to covet honour,

I am the most offending soul alive. ◄———— **Pathos:** 'no stomach' evokes shame and cowardice

Rather proclaim it, Westmorland, through my host,

That he which hath no stomach to this fight, ◄————

Let him depart; his passport shall be made, **Ethos:** Henry shows some humility but also his commitment to patriotism

And crowns for convoy put into his purse;

We would not die in that man's company

That fears his felllowship to die with us.

This day is call'd the feast of Crispian.

He that outlives this day, and comes safe home,

Will stand a tip-toe when this day is nam'd,

And rouse him at the name of Crispian.

He that shall see this day, and live old age,

Will yearly on the vigil feast his neighbours,

And say 'Tomorrow is Saint Crispian.'

Then will he strip his sleeve and show his scars, **Pathos:** Henry wants us to feel proud and as if we've been given a rare and precious gift.

And say 'These wounds I had on Crispin's day.'

This story shall the good man teach his son;

We few, we happy few, we band of brothers; **Ethos:** Henry wants us to believe that he is willing to sacrifice himself.

For he today that sheds his blood with me

Shall be my brother; be he ne'er so vile,

This day shall gentle his condition; **Logos:** Henry wants us to think that being out-numbered is actually advantageous as the soldiers will be more respected.

And gentlemen in England now a-bed

Shall think themselves accurs'd they were not here,

And hold their manhoods cheap whiles any speaks

That fought with us upon Saint Crispin's day.

---

15. Shakespeare, W. (2015) *Henry V.* Oxford: Oxford University Press.

I'll ask students to make a note of the rhetorical triangle on the extract. Once they've found an appeal to at least two of ethos, pathos or logos, they've got the main thrust of the extract. This increases confidence and gives them something to look for specifically in the text. It helps that Shakespeare usually introduces the most important themes of a speech in the first lines, with the rest of the speech repeating and developing this. In the example above, we've identified three strands to Henry's argument, so students could now find further evidence of these strands, giving them a focus as they read on. The mass of language is reduced to something manageable in this way.

Examining the text in this way also means students can craft a triple thesis opening for their extended essays. The thesis is the idea explored in the essay. One thesis is usually not rich enough to allow students to explore in depth, but three gives them more potential and provides more direction. The question might be: 'How is honour presented in Henry V?' Students could open their essay by briefly explaining how the rhetorical triangle has been used: *Shakespeare uses Henry V to portray honour in a variety of ways. It is presented as a rare gift for which we should be grateful; something that even the most privileged people desire and as a source of self-respect.* Students can then think about elsewhere in the play where these representations reoccur.

We can also borrow the concept of 'kairos', which relates to timing. It's difficult to pin down but equates to discussing the right topics at the right time. Students can work out the big themes of the time through reading the text itself, rather than learning about context first. That is, we shouldn't really need to be told before reading *A Taste of Honey* that being gay was seen as taboo in the 1950s. This comes across in the presentation of Geof and how others see him. Essentially, if the text considers the theme, *it's relevant to the time.* This means that we don't have to teach discrete and time-consuming history lessons before embarking on a text.

The rhetorical triangle is an advantageous device for both analysing a text and writing up the analysis. It can also be employed when students write their own opinion pieces.

Strategy: Hot reading	
Good for…	**Sub-strategies**
• **Re-reads**	• Power games
• Deepening inference	• All is allegory
• Preparing for unseen texts	• Text as teacher
• Analysis/evaluation	• Time machine
• Comparing perspectives	• Rhetorical triangle
• Close reading of extracts	

Once students are proficient cold and hot readers, the hardest work is done. *We're always better off teaching how to read than how to read a specific text.*

Strategy 2: Cold reading (the text is unknown)		
What?	**How?**	**Why?**
• **Equipping students for how to read any new texts.** • Teaching students to read interactively from the beginning.	• Show students the **reading continuum**. • Teach students **Labov's narrative model**. • For confident students, condense Labov's narrative model to the **Follow my leader** framework and focus on conflict and changes. • Teach the common patterns of **power and conflict**. • Consolidate with some knowledge of characterisation/motivation.	• To prepare students to read anything, anywhere. • Makes them confident readers on the unseen section (AO1). • Means that even set texts don't have to be studied in forensic detail to be appreciated. • Overcomes barriers like infrequent school attendance and poor memory, as students can comment meaningfully even when set texts are unfamiliar (AO1).
Strategy 2: Hot reading (the text is becoming familiar)		
• **Teaching students to re-read texts critically.** • Helping students to start analysing the content.	• Refer students to the reading continuum and the **transformative capabilities of re-reading**. • Build on the cold strategies by asking **why/how** questions. • Consider texts as **allegories** and excavate possible meanings. • Clarify what the text wants to **teach the reader**. • Link to the constant **big ideas of societies, past and present**.	• Provides a framework for analytical explorations that build on cold reading strategies. • Enables richer readings of unseen and pre-studied texts. • Makes it explicit that texts are a construct. • Establishes the special skills of literary criticism, as opposed to 'just reading'. • Prepares students to be writers too because they can think of their own texts as 'lessons' to an audience. What is it they want to teach the world?

It helps to keep showing students the reading continuum as they develop their skills and add strategies, and to remind them of the need for different types of reading.

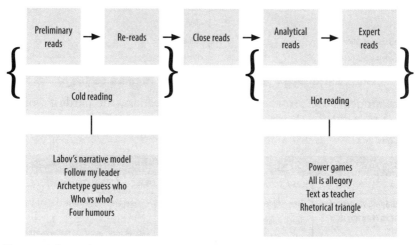

Figure 5: The reading continuum with strategies

STRATEGY 3: THE MATRIX

WHAT?

Once you've provided your students with a range of reading strategies, you can begin to focus on the specific texts of the Literature papers. But how can so much text, background knowledge and language technique be condensed?

Many teachers do prefer their students to read texts in their entirety. I'll admit, I think it's *almost* inadequate not to. Yet, there are so many demands on our students' time that it now seems immoral to crowd their learning time in this way when basic literacy might require more attention.

Looking at matrices in texts is a method that can help save us time. **A matrix is the origin of political, sociological and cultural ideas.** All texts contain matrices as all texts contain ideas.

It is possible to identify a text's matrices, match quotations to them and then focus most of your teaching on these models rather than on reading the whole text. Five matrices for *Macbeth* are included later on, but Figure 6 gives one example to show how quotations have been organised to create the matrix of 'blood' in *Macbeth*.

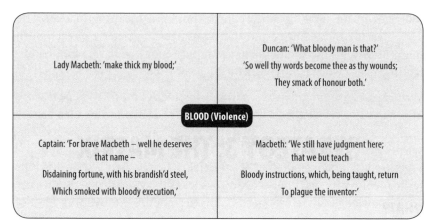

Figure 6: 'Blood' matrix for *Macbeth*

WHY?

In my lessons, matrices have been used to compact texts, develop literary analysis and even support essay writing. They have also helped me not to over-differentiate. Greg Ashman explores how differentiation can actually *prevent* students from learning as well as they can in *Education Myths*.[16] Once I was aware of this, I needed a way to stop myself from thinking of parts of the text as challenging and non-challenging, and of over-preparing some classes by endlessly breaking down extracts at the expense of honing their written responses.

Focusing on matrices means that students of all abilities have the chance to explore the text in the same way. Consequently, LPA students are more likely to make richer inferences because they are exposed to more complex quotations. However, they aren't overwhelmed because the matrices are naturally succinct. Conversely, HPA students have to dig deeper into the more 'obvious' quotations to excavate original responses, so they are forced to employ a broader range of reading strategies, preventing complacency.

---

16. Ashman, G. (2019) 'The Differentiation Myth' in Bennett, T. (ed.) *Education Myths*. Woodbridge: John Catt.

Matrices mean texts can be reduced but in a meaningful way. They don't overtax the memory and they can meet the criteria of each of the literature AOs. Once students have an outline of the basic plot of a text, reading every word is rarely the best use of time.

Writers can use language as matrices for ideas and often repeat words or images to explore them. I was particularly drawn to this idea because it links to Piaget's theory that the brain builds schemas to recall knowledge.[17] Schemas are mental frameworks where information is organised. The construction of effective schemas is essential for long-term memory as old knowledge provides the basis for new knowledge. New knowledge, therefore, needs to have something it can link to or it's likely to be forgotten. This can be ameliorated by helping students to build new schemas.

As you can see on pages 64-66, matrices mimic schemas. Frequently, teachers use mind-maps or spider diagrams to help students build schemas, but these can often be confusing and overwhelming. Matrices mean that students understand the importance of a theme, hang quotations on it, use this to craft inferences, then stretch these inferences by using a range of syntax to help them explain further. We can build layers of skills on the matrices as well as using them to gather key quotations. If a text is new to a student (i.e. they have no schema to build upon) then this method works very well. In effect, students are uncovering a key theme and then stacking the evidence for it on the matrix.

HOW?

Many of my students struggled during lockdown as we studied *Macbeth* because not all students could attend every remote lesson. I caught them up not by going over plot summaries or showing the film, but by presenting a matrix. That is, I explained that the play uses the image of blood repeatedly. I asked questions such as: What can they predict about the play? Where is Shakespeare directing their attention? Where have they seen blood imagery before?

---

17. Piaget, J. (1952) *The Origins of Intelligence in Children*. New York: International University Press.

We then looked at the scene with the Captain (Act 1, Scene 2). Students were able to understand his speech much more quickly as it linked to the schema they'd begun to build on Macbeth's character through the blood matrix. They could also see the Captain was presenting us with an ideal of masculinity, so I was then able to present the 'man' matrix to them to exhibit how the man motif is used elsewhere in the play. In one early lesson, they'd looked at the text as a whole.

I give students copies of the matrices in booklets to refer to in class and for revision. You can print one matrix on each sheet so that students can organise inferences and thesis statements around them. They can also be printed on A3 and students can write an essay or plan on the sheet itself. The matrix is not only there to represent the writer's ideas but also to direct the student's response. This illustrates to them that their essay is really part of a dialogue with the writer. The writer presents an image of blood and so the reader replies.

Matrices are useful when comparing texts too. It's often taxing enough when students have to understand, recall and analyse one text. When they have to hold this information in their head as they make links to another text, it can be overwhelming. If students are comparing matrices rather than texts, they have less strain on their memory and are able to see links more clearly. So I might shrink the poem 'Storm on the Island' to the matrices of 'blows', 'sea' and 'nothing'. I could distil the poem 'Exposure' into 'nothing', 'winds' and 'dying.' The use of savage natural imagery to hint at mental or social turbulence is apparent immediately without analysing every line. Students have now created a schema on which to build their comparisons.

I uncovered the idea of matrices when reading Frank Kermode's *Shakespeare's Language*. Kermode noticed that Shakespeare repeats certain words frequently in his plays. Kermode discovered this as he'd been annoyed that much discussion of the Bard ignores his status as master poet and so ignores the *power of the language*. By focusing on the poetry, Kermode discovered five matrices in Macbeth: time, man, done, blood and darkness.[18] I collected quotations around these matrices for

---

18. Kermode, F. (2001) *Shakespeare's Language*. Penguin.

my classes and also paired each key word with an overarching idea that will likely link to any possible exam question.

You can create your own matrices for Macbeth if you feel your students will respond better, but I've used Kermode's and found them abundant enough for students to get a full picture of the play's themes. You could have students identify the matrices from a limited number of extracts if you do want them to be involved in some way. In an ideal world, we'd read the full text with our students and then create matrices, but this is unrealistic. I find if teachers prepare the matrices themselves, it saves time for more important skills than quotation gathering.

Ultimately, the matrix is a way to make sure that students are focusing on exploring and explaining the significant language of the play and not being distracted by extraneous contextual information. The matrices are more meaningful than quote banks because the quotations are linked to central images that link to key themes. Many teachers complain that students neglect the language of the text in their essays: they're able to make some great inferences and display sound knowledge of Jacobean politics, but this isn't desirable unless students *explain the techniques that have sent these messages* or raised the issues in the first place.

Reiterated words or images are apparent in the other plays too – indeed in all texts by all writers. If you want to build your own matrices, you can simply read a text and highlight the repeated words, collecting the most apposite quotations around them. Most matrices are likely to be built on nouns and verbs. The matrices could end up being quite large, so we can be circumspect when deciding which quotations to collate.

I've applied the matrix method to modern texts like *DNA*. Here 'laugh', 'Adam' 'dead', 'you' and 'we' dominate. The prefix 'every' is frequent too. Pronouns might be words you ordinarily avoid, as these will be very frequent as the building blocks of sentences, but in a play about gangs and the individual versus the group, pronouns can be very telling. In fact, this list is really revealing. When I showed this list of words to a class it immediately got them thinking about the themes of the play; we began to create schemas so that when they looked at the play in more detail they were more likely to understand and recall it later on. (This is especially important when students aren't presented with an extract from the text in the exam.) Some students were able to spot the theme of sacrifice from the juxtaposition of these words even before we'd begun hot reading, and they'd learnt some quotations almost without effort.

You may find you can predict the most repeated language in the texts, and you can go back to quote banks and sort those into matrices if a complete re-read is impractical. I much prefer the term 'matrix' to 'quote bank' because it reminds students that texts create and comment on ideas, so their analysis must respond to these ideas. 'Quote bank' suggests we make a withdrawal, shove it in our essay and so have engaged with the text. Not so. I've always found that mind-maps look impressive but are difficult to use quickly and to visualise in the memory. I'm also not so keen on students annotating the texts in great detail. This works for some students but many write so much that the text is even *more* intimidating! The matrices are a cleaner way to organise and limit ideas. Limiting ideas might seem odd, but we know that students often veer from the focus of a question. This can be because they're trying to explicate too many references.

Here are a few examples of matrices that could be used for other Shakespeare plays:

- *Hamlet* = father, man, time, think, heaven, mother, love

- *Othello* = villain, love, sacrifice, gift, lips

- *Romeo and Juliet* = love, death, night, man, kiss

- *The Tempest* = monster, human, spirit, strange, love

It is possible to collect quotes that hang on just a few matrices and still teach a play meaningfully. Indeed, students can apply a broader range of cold and hot reading techniques to the quotes in the matrices as the amount of text is more controlled. In some of my past lessons, students have moved along the length of the reading continuum in less than 15 minutes because they're focusing on slivers of the text. They can move on from understanding that Macbeth is a violent character in the 'blood' matrix to giving different interpretations swiftly. One of my classes uncovered that Macbeth could be seen as a radical freedom fighter if we see his violence as an allegory for rebellion and if we don't consider his violence as against people but against systems. This kind of deep inference usually takes lessons, not minutes. Matrices have accelerated this greatly.

By understanding the ideas that hang on the words in the matrices and by learning a limited number of quotations, students are beginning to satisfy AO1 and AO2 of the Literature criteria. Context (AO3) is inherent in the matrix itself as students know a matrix is the origin of political, cultural and sociological ideas. That is, if the matrix is 'man' then this is going to link to masculinity, status and power. If it's 'done' then we can link to free will versus control, etc. Whatever the questions, the matrices will always be useful because they can be bent to link to any theme.

Additionally, using matrices rather than full texts and long extracts can increase AO4 skills, because it will leave more time to craft analytical and evaluative syntax. We'll return there soon.

HOW?[19]

In the first lesson on *Macbeth*, I show students the key words from the matrices (time, man, done, blood and darkness) and we jot down general ideas and predictions. Here we have our schema that we'll begin to build on.

We'll then read a plot summary. I like to pause and ask how our five key words might be linking to events, characters, etc. Are our first ideas still relevant?

Once students can recall the plot and have some knowledge of character roles, the matrices can be re-introduced in more detail. I look at an extract from the play about once a week, but refer to the matrices in every lesson. We might look at one matrix per lesson and discuss our inferences. Students might be split into groups to report back on the different matrices. We might take one quote from each matrix and explore how they link together. Instead of spending an hour in the lesson reading an Act, we parse the matrix quotations repeatedly but with longer gaps between to build recall. I print matrices with parts missing that students have to complete from memory. I've spent many hours making impressive looking worksheets but their uses were finite. The matrix sheets can be used in many different ways.

---

19. Shakespeare, W. (1992) *Macbeth*. Wordsworth Editions.

Once we'd got to know the plot of *Macbeth*, I began deeper analysis with my students by showing them the 'darkness' matrix. We 'exploded' each of the quotations, i.e. looked closely at each image, giving alternative interpretations and connotations. Then we examined the opening with the witches. My students not only commented on the witches in this scene but were able to see parallels with Lady Macbeth, even though we hadn't yet looked a scene in which she appears.

Students were then able to write a short response to 'How are women presented in the play?' Moving on to a written response so quickly in literature is rare. In the past it's edged towards the three-week mark because of reading, watching, discussing, annotating, etc. The matrix approach meant students could write meaningfully about two of the most important characters in the first week. Students didn't struggle to begin either because they knew to open with reference to the motifs of the matrix ('Women are presented through the motif of darkness.') They knew their ideas would develop so rather than endlessly annotating texts, students went back to earlier responses and added new insights or developed an inference by trying out a different sentence structure. The matrix allows you to balance close reading with analytical writing right from the start of the SOW. Quote banks certainly don't.

Figures 7–11 show example matrices for Act 1 of Macbeth.

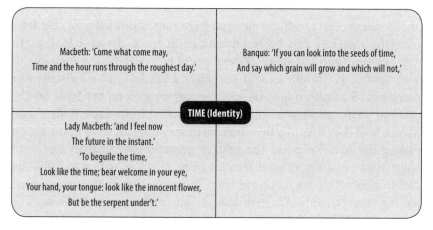

Figure 7: 'Time' matrix for *Macbeth*

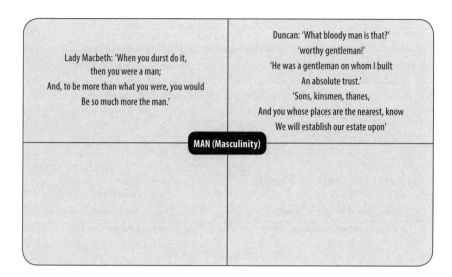

Figure 8: 'Man' matrix for *Macbeth*

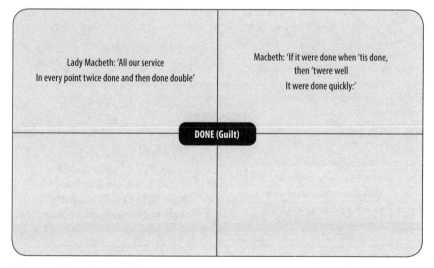

Figure 9: 'Done' matrix for *Macbeth*

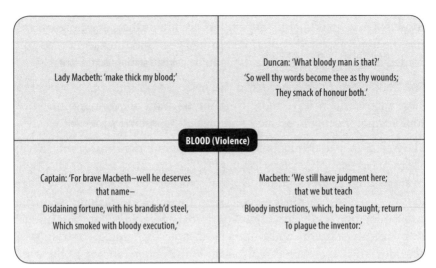

Figure 10: 'Blood' matrix for *Macbeth*

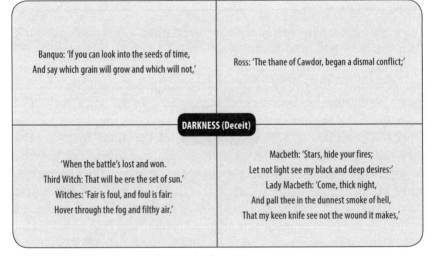

Figure 11: 'Darkness' matrix for *Macbeth*

It is evident that the key themes (ambition, equivocation, manipulation) are still apparent but I was intrigued by some of the twists that occurred. Interestingly, Duncan becomes a stronger presence (he has five of the quotations, going beyond the usual 'He was a man on whom I built an absolute trust', making him appear less credulous than we've presumed), and the underexplored quotations shine. I've found the matrix made me excited about the play again as I began to consider neglected areas.

The quotes and their concepts in the matrices are multi-use. Compiling these matrices can leave more time for thinking, developing inference, applying hot reading to extracts and mastering a convincing written style.

The next step is to think about how we can more richly satisfy the needs of language analysis. A later strategy ('The big five') looks at the high-leverage language techniques to teach, but here we can see how we can *control* the technical terms being identified. Often students will dive into a quotation and begin to pull out verbs and nouns, but these are not always the most useful, and while a close focus on a single word can raise new ideas, this approach can also lead to misunderstanding as the word isn't linked back to the sentence in which it appears. Using the matrix means that we can teach students that a text's messages are conveyed through symbols.

For instance, students might explicate the phrase 'When you durst do it, then you were a man.' Often they will zoom in on 'man' and say it has connotations of strength, but they haven't looked at how Lady Macbeth has weaponised this word. Some students might say that Lady Macbeth wants her husband to be stronger because she uses the noun 'man'. This is getting better but hasn't really oriented the quote in the play as a whole. Once students know that 'man' is a key symbol, they know that whenever they find the word it will have a metaphorical use: it will not just be a comment on Macbeth but wider society. Now students can explore how Lady Macbeth uses 'man' to attack her husband and his undeserved patriarchal power. For Lady Macbeth, 'man' is a symbol of her resentment as she has not been granted this status. The matrices help here because you can teach five symbols – mostly nouns – that function as metaphors to illuminate society. We don't need to spend hours drumming in the differences between adjectives and adverbs, etc.

Immediately, students can open their essays with a focus on symbols, motifs, repetition, imagery and semantic fields (all technical terms meaning a group of repeated words). Students begin with language and so are more likely to keep the focus of their essay on language too. The above terms are high leverage because they can be manipulated to help explain structural choices as well. For example, what imagery dominates in the opening? How and why does this change by the end? Explaining the *purpose* of the technique gathers marks and is fundamentally analysis, whilst highlighting any number of adjectives and verbs most definitely isn't. If students learn the matrix, they learn the language features too.

In Figure 12, you can see how a matrix can be used to blend AO1 and AO2 in a thesis statement (the opening of an essay that sets out the central idea or thesis that the essay will focus on). Whatever the examiner asks, it can be linked back to the concepts in the matrices.

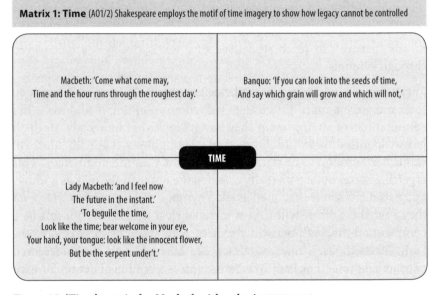

Matrix 1: Time (AO1/2) Shakespeare employs the motif of time imagery to show how legacy cannot be controlled

Macbeth: 'Come what come may,
Time and the hour runs through the roughest day.'

Banquo: 'If you can look into the seeds of time,
And say which grain will grow and which will not,'

TIME

Lady Macbeth: 'and I feel now
The future in the instant.'
'To beguile the time,
Look like the time; bear welcome in your eye,
Your hand, your tongue: look like the innocent flower,
But be the serpent under't.'

Figure 12: 'Time' matrix for *Macbeth* with a thesis statement

It's plain how students can learn opening statements that identify a writer's methods and messages, and hint at the bigger ideas. For example, if the question is 'How does Shakespeare present the theme of ambition?', the answer can begin '*Shakespeare employs the motif of time imagery to show how ambition is ultimately futile because we cannot control our legacy as our power is fleeting.*' Here, I've opened with a technique, a mention of the writer's intention and the bigger themes of legacy and power. With this statement a student will have made a confident start, as inference, language and context are set out in the opening. The student knows they need to explain this in detail so have set themselves a secure path, and essays that open well are much less likely to flounder.

We can sometimes feel powerless as literature teachers as we feel there's some luck involved with the question that arises in the exam, but this approach shows we have power over how our students begin and continue their answer, and how we can bend the question to suit the matrices or ideas they've learnt. Whether they're asked about ambition, the supernatural or betrayal in *Macbeth* doesn't matter, as the five matrices comment on all of these things. For example, supernatural can be explored through the matrix of 'man' as this undermines masculine power. Character questions can be framed by reference to the matrices too, as in this example: '*Macbeth is presented through the repetition of time images to show his obsession with status, ambition and being ill-used by fate.*' Again, there's mention of language and its effects in the opening of the essay. It's unlikely now for students not to make other insightful comments on the text.

Contextual understanding needs to be developed next, and matrices can help us with this too. There isn't time for students to learn the politics and intrigues of the early Jacobean Age. In fact, this kind of knowledge tends to overshadow the language on the page and force students into the obvious, with observations like '*Macbeth is shocking because he wants to be king. This is naughty because the Great Chain of Being says he can't.*'

Instead, if we teach our students about the general nature of power, conflict and rebellion, we can keep the inferences broad enough for each student to be imaginative but still relevant and text-focused. 'Who vs who?' on page 35 is one way to do this.

'Power games' (page 43) will have also shown students that status linked to class, race and gender is at the root of all texts and they can explicate how a character feels about their status. Ultimately, characters are either questioning or accepting of their status. And their dissatisfactions will come from their relationship to the big three: class, race and gender.

Macbeth is class-obsessed! Figure 13 shows how we could develop a matrix to allow for an exploration of power (a near synonym for context in GCSE Literature).

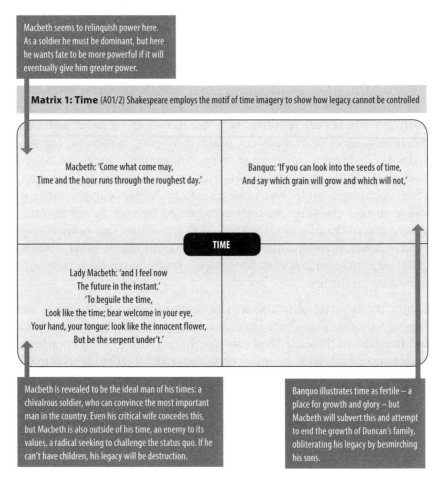

Figure 13: 'Time' matrix for *Macbeth* with an exploration of power

The context of *Macbeth* relies more on a thorough understanding of the plot than knowing James I seemed a bit too keen on witches. Family, legacy and the brevity of life will be topics of literature past, present and to come, so we can talk about big ideas without frittering time on 'context carousels' and 'marketplaces'. It's also a bit rich to be frustrated when students discuss history more than the text itself if we begin with a 'dump' of contextual information, as we're signifying this is the most important learning above the text itself. Moreover, in Mccrea's report, research supports that a student's 'understanding arises through connection'.[20] The matrices present a range of quotations from different parts of the text so students have to work out how they link together and how they delineate the big ideas or contextual themes. They are unlikely to attend to a mass of facts about Elizabethans if there is nothing from the text to link it to.

[B] Five sentence structures

So far, we've seen how a matrix can reduce a text, focus on the language, remove the need for rote learning of techniques and allow for context to be at the heart of inference. Next we need to think about how a matrix can support the writing of an essay itself and AO4. By spending less time re-reading the set texts and learning generalised and sketchy details of Jacobean (or Victorian, or Georgian etc.) life, we can take time to think about how to craft a literary analysis. This allows us to prepare for the writing of analysis on the Language papers too.

By becoming familiar with the five sentence structures in the table below, students will make their writing not only clearer but more open and flexible to catch a range of inferences.[21] Lemov advised that we 'front the writing'.[22] This means that we don't leave the essay to the end of the lesson after discussing, reading, discussing some more, etc. Because we can make use of matrices, we can now 'front' the writing more quickly and easily.

Firstly, students must be aware that phrases do different jobs (where a phrase equals a unit of meaning within the sentence).

20. Mccrea, P. (2019) *Learning: What Is It and How Might We Catalyse It?* Ambition Institute.

21. Tom Needham's *Writing Skills in Literacy – An Evidence-Informed Guide for Teachers* first drew my attention to the possibilities of appositive and participial phrases.

22. Lemov, D. (2015) *Teach Like a Champion*. San Francisco: Josey Bass.

Phrase	Good for...	Example
1. The noun phrase – the noun and all that modifies (gives details to) it.	• Capturing inferences clearly. • LPA students who struggle to articulate in multiclausal sentences. • Evaluating quotes. • Embedding quotes. • Smuggling in context 'buzzwords'.	The **subversive play** *Macbeth* seems to celebrate rebellion. The **disturbing phrase** 'Come what come may' hints at Macbeth's fatalistic attitude.
2. The **verb phrase** – the verb and all that modifies it.	• Capturing changes in characters. • Showing a response to the whole text. • Evaluating events.	Macbeth is **eager to please** King Duncan before his mind **is cruelly infected**. (This shows Macbeth's transformation but also offers a *judgement* on what has happened.)
3. **Infinitive verb phrase** – using the 'to' form of a verb.	• Explaining effects of language. • Summarising information. • Blending with embedded quotes.	**To create an atmosphere of doom**, Shakespeare embeds a series of inescapable images, e.g. blood and darkness. Shakespeare uses Macbeth's soliloquy **to reveal his 'vaulting ambition' is really at the root of his transgression**.
4. **Appositive phrase** – restates and defines a noun.	• Allowing for more inference. • By definition, it shows interpretation. • A more fluid way of including a range of inferences. • Moving beyond merely repeating an explicit comment on the text. • Showing similarities/differences.	Macbeth, **a man of ruthless ambition**, will not be constrained by Christian morality. **A woman of remarkable assurance**, Lady Macbeth is not a submissive wife.
5. **Participial phrase** – participles show the tense a verb is happening in.	• Making evaluative comments. • Illustrating that literature is happening *now*. • Explaining the effects of language.	**Speaking in a resigned tone**, Macbeth shows he will not fight against the witches' prophecy. **Using the motif of time** allows Shakespeare to illustrate that man 'frets his hour upon the stage' in vain.

These phrases can be utilised when students produce their own writing and analyses in the Language papers. They can also be useful when feeding back to students by equipping them with explicit strategies for improvement. For example, if a student's inference is too obvious, ask them to move from a noun phrase to an appositive phrase, thereby satisfying more of the AOs and creating a useful shorthand for marking.

If the question is 'How does Shakespeare present Macbeth?', a student might have answered: *Ambitious Macbeth killed the king because he wants power*. This is the beginning of an inference but by combining with an appositive, students are forced to justify their inference further: *Ambitious Macbeth, a man driven to kill the king, is insecure in in his masculinity*. We've now moved to three inferences: Macbeth is ambitious; this is why he kills the king (more so than because his wife tells him to!); he's also insecure. We have a complex sentence too, which lends sophistication to the answer.

If a student hasn't supported this with any textual reference, you can then advise them to add an infinitive verb phrase. For example: *To illustrate Macbeth's insecurity, the play is littered with the motif of man: from Duncan's 'worthy gentleman' to Lady Macbeth's 'more than a man,' all the characters present a masculine ideal to Macbeth that he fears he cannot match*. The matrix supports this approach because students can go back and practise explaining the metaphor of 'darkness' or 'man' etc. through these different phrases. You don't always have to spend time on extracts before practising the writing of the analysis. The matrices provide some quick inferences so students can focus on syntax.

To help students learn these sentence types, I usually teach them in pairs:

1. Noun phrase and appositive phrase.

2. Verb phrase and infinitive verb phrase.

3. Participial phrase linking back to a noun phrase (*Speaking in a resigned tone, fatalistic Macbeth shows he will not fight against the manipulative witches' prophecy.*)

I begin with an example of a sentence on the board and ask students to break the sentence down into its chunks of information. This is really helpful as students are often taught that a sentence is a piece of information, whereas many sentences are a chain of information. For example:

The subversive play Macbeth seems to celebrate rebellion.

Students will, of course, isolate that the play is subversive and rebellious. I then rewrite the sentence to keep the key information only: Macbeth *is subversive and rebellious.*

I ask students to explain which sentence they prefer. Invariably it is the first. We discuss why and students are usually able to comment on how the phrases split the information up. If they don't prefer the better-phrased example, we also discuss this but I ask: Which sentence would the examiner prefer? This gets the necessary response!

Now I'll explain the particular phrase types employed. Students then need to see me crafting examples. I'll refer to the matrices and say I'll use one of the phrases (such as the noun phrase) to explain the significance of the blood motif. Students are already familiar with these inferences so their attention is not split between following the inference and following the creation of the phrase itself.

Next, I might create a 'cloze' sentence (a sentence with key words missing) and have students direct me on how to complete it. I'll employ the 'I do, we do, you do' sequence until students are practising the construction completely independently. We'll then add this sentence structure to our success criteria for literary essays. The students also go back to their matrix and write examples of the phrase type around the motif. The schema is fired again, so students are now adding grammatical knowledge to plot, quote and inference understanding.

Other ways you can encourage proficiency are:

- Finding examples of these sentence structures in the texts themselves.

- Breaking class discussion up by occasionally saying something like: 'We've heard Jo's comments on violence in the play. Everybody summarise these on the blood matrix with a verb phrase. Can you develop this idea with an appositive phrase?'

- Inserting the sentences into writing scaffolds.

- Asking students to rewrite model responses by adding in the phrases, to help clarify and expand on the ideas.

- Placing new vocabulary in the sentence structures.

- Asking students to rephrase using a particular sentence type when giving verbal answers.

- Students rewriting the learning objectives using one of the phrases.

- Linking back to hot and cold reading. Students might use 'Follow my leader' (page 33) and note down initial ideas in simple sentences. (A simple sentence contains one subject and one verb.) When they re-read, I'll ask them to go back to their 'Follow my leader' notes. Can they add a noun phrase to the opening of the simple sentence? What inferences are they now creating?

- Explaining to students that learning a range of phrases is a cold writing technique – that is, students can practise these phrases and use them with whatever topic they're asked to write about. Again we're showing students they can revise English beyond learning ten quotations from *Pride and Prejudice*.

It can help students if they use the phrases with topics they know really well, especially if they struggle to recall the different phrases. I've had students describe their weekend using the phrases. One student, a keen cook, used to explain recipes to me with different phrases.

I find shorter exercises work best for grammar. However, we can make AO4 a prime focus of essays from time to time now we've used the matrices to lessen the need for reading whole texts. I might pose a simple question such as 'How does Shakespeare present violence?' Students should be primed to link the question back to the matrices. They'll look mostly at the 'blood' matrix so will have quotations and some inferences ready to use. I'll ask them to include particular phrases and then will mark the essay purely for AO4. This can seem very time-consuming (though it can be done with self and peer assessment), but I've discovered that poor inferences are more often poor because they're framed in limiting sentence structures, rather than because the student doesn't understand the text. Look at the examples below. Essentially, the inference is the same; it's the expression that impresses rather than the idea.

Macbeth uses violence to get what he wants.

Frustrated Macbeth, a previously admired soldier, is sadly driven to violence by his 'vaulting ambition'.

We're not going to improve a student's inferences by simply reading the whole text or copying a handful of key quotes onto a hand-out. When students have grasped the ideas of the matrices, know some quotations and the themes they link to, then we have to think about how best to use this knowledge – not shove more of the original text at them. Inevitability, some students are not going to get beyond the more obvious ideas, but we can make these ideas shine brighter by setting them in better sentences.

USING PHRASES TO BUILD ANALYTICAL PARAGRAPHS

The five phrases above can also provide scaffolding and frameworks for less confident students. Admittedly, such frameworks can become tiresome and limiting. There are times I'd wish PEE would P off, but we can't escape the fact that any essay, however sophisticated, is ultimately a main point supported by evidence that is analysed and responded to – PEAR. If students know this to be a *general* rather than prescriptive shape, it should be a flexible skeleton.

Let's imagine our exam question: '*How does the play Macbeth* present morality?'

Part of the essay	Phrase	Example
Opening – thesis statement. (If well-crafted, this stands as a plan. The modifications to the noun will be the central points of later paragraphs.) (Appositive phrases offer greater immediate satisfaction of the AOs, but do not provide as clear a roadmap as noun phrases.)	Noun phrase. Appositive phrase.	*The Tragedy of Macbeth* is a **powerful, radical play** that uses a range of motifs to explore the **fluid, contradictory and constraining nature** of morality. *The Tragedy of Macbeth*, **a play fascinated by the interpretation of right and wrong**, uses motifs to illustrate that a shared view of morality is the glue of social cohesion.
First point – fluid morality.	Vary the opening each new point with noun phrases or appositives. (AO1) Use verbs to begin to explain the effects of language. (AO2) Develop with a participial phrase. (AO3) It can help to make a summative statement by beginning with an adverb to reveal the audience reaction. (AO3) AO4 should be developing alongside the ideas.	Morality, the driving theme of this turbulent play, is fluid: 'fair is foul and foul is fair'. To suggest the nebulous nature of right and wrong, Shakespeare employs a confusing paradoxical phrase. Confusing the audience is a way to force us to question the values we simply accept; we have to see that right and wrong are personal perceptions and can actually be a force for chaos in society. Ironically, the witches – a disenfranchised group of women – are shown to have a sophisticated, if subversive, understanding of social control: they know that the tighter the controls, the more radical the rebellion.
Second point – contradictory morality.	Use a similar structure but vary the phrases. E.g. summarise with a verb phrase.	Moreover, the frustrating constraints of medieval society force Lady Macbeth into rebellion: 'look like the innocent flower but be the serpent under 't.' The juxtaposition of 'flower' and 'serpent' is to draw attention again to the paradoxes of nature. Using these images tells us that even nature had good and evil so denying them is futile. Daringly, Shakespeare alludes to biblical imagery to remind us that good exists only because evil does. Macbeth teaches us to understand the interdependency of right and wrong.

Third point – constraining morality.	Now explain the third thesis. Try opening with an adverbial phrase. Beginning a sentence with a prepositional phrase can also help to expand on structural analysis and show an overview of the text.	Intriguingly, Macbeth is not presented unsympathetically. Macbeth, a murderous tyrant, also provokes empathy, showing the contradictory nature of morality. Speaking in a weary but regretful tone, Macbeth laments: 'blood will have blood'. Seeing the image of gore reminds the audience of the outrage on Duncan, but also hints at the cyclical nature of violence and revenge. Even conservative Macduff, a supposed hero, is part of the cycle of revenge. From the opening, Macbeth seems caught in a web of fate. At the close, this is made clear by Macduff's brutality. 'Fair and foul' appear to be shifting again.
Closing – return to the central thesis.	Begin with a participial phrase.	Using the motifs of moral fluidity and contradictions has allowed Shakespeare to illustrate that morality is in the eye of the beholder. Macbeth is the 'fair' radical challenging a status quo that constrains through fear and religion; Macbeth is also 'foul,' a tyrant who murders to sustain his own regime. Therefore, the moral 'fog' is not ever penetrated, showing that we cannot have an absolute sense of good.

We can now see how focusing on matrices allows us to polish inferences as well as writing skills. Using the matrices means that students move on to responding to the text more quickly, rather than simply consuming the text.

Using matrices will speed up understanding of plots and key themes, leaving more time to practise inference and analysis of language. Furthermore, if students already have mastery of cold and hot reading, they will be equipped to tackle longer extracts and to link them more broadly to the entire text.

Above we've reduced *Macbeth* to five matrices, but you could go further than this. In the Appendix, I've reduced each AQA poem to just three matrices. For example, for 'Bayonet Charge' the matrices could be 'running,' rifle' and 'charge'. I consider 'running' and 'rifle' to be the main ones: 'Running' hints at the soldier's abandoning of blind patriotism, whilst 'rifle' is both the tool of his potential destruction but also the object that alerts him to his futility and vulnerability.

Why not make different members of staff responsible for creating the matrices you use? One alert, deep read of the text can save hours or planning, resource making and printing.

Strategy 3: The matrix		
What?	How?	Why?
• A matrix is the origin of political, social and cultural ideas. • Texts use repeated images or phrases that create these matrices. • Students focus on the language of the matrices rather than the whole text.	• Use Kermode's existing matrices or create your own to suit students' needs. • Employ **spaced learning** (strategy 6) to instil plot comprehension. • Focus teaching and learning on quotations within the matrix. • Apply **cold and hot reading** strategies to increase comprehension and analysis. • Demonstrate how each stage of the matrix matches an assessment objective. • Move from quote analysis to matching big ideas to the matrix. • Use **buzzwords** (strategy 4) to support generic but rich ideas. • Develop students' writing by applying rehearsed phrases that support whole-text analysis.	• Speeds up basic comprehension to progress quickly from plot recall to understanding (A01). • Provides a schema to support memory (A01/2/3/4). • Sharply focuses analysis on language itself (A02). • Draws attention to patterns and structures as well as language (A02). • Allows progression from language analysis to how language supports exploration of ideologies (A03). • Leaves time for crafting analytical writing itself (A04).

STRATEGY 4: BUZZWORDS

WHAT?

In order to make wider comments on society and politics for AO3, students need a lexicon: a collection of terms that could describe any age, theme or character. Alex Quigley's *Closing the Vocabulary Gap* made me aware of my misconception that if students were in school being exposed to sophisticated language then they must be learning/understanding it too.[23] Like any other skill, vocabulary has to be discretely taught. Again, this can take a lot of time and then we have to build opportunities for students to use new lexis repeatedly. This can seem overwhelming but there are solutions.

Quigley discusses 'nominalisation' too.[24] This is the process of turning a high-frequency verb into a low-frequency noun. For example, 'looking on the downside' becomes 'pessimism'. The tone of the writing is more scholarly and also more concise.

Embarrassingly, I once planned to explicitly teach some higher vocabulary to my class at the beginning of a *Macbeth* SOW, but when it came to the first lesson I omitted it, as I thought it was too difficult and not necessary. Further into the SOW, I set the class an essay task on *Macbeth* asking about the witches. One student stared into space for ten minutes. I directed him towards his writing scaffold, sentence starters, etc. but he still did not begin. I asked him to give me some ideas about the witches

---

23. Quigley, A. (2018) *Closing the Vocabulary Gap*. Routlegde.
24. Quigley, A. 'How Can We Develop Vocabulary in the Classroom?' in Murphy, J. (ed.) *The ResearchED Guide to Literacy*. John Catt.

and I'd jot them down for him. He said, 'I know what I want to say but it seems wrong. The witches are liars but not liars.' He had identified equivocation. He was a student with SEND but was perspicacious enough to detect this. However, I was stupid enough to have rejected the word for explicit teaching.

That was an epiphany for me. If I'd trusted in explicit vocabulary instruction to help students define, label and express ideas, he'd have been equipped with the sophisticated nominalisation 'equivocation' rather than the woolly verb phrase 'sort of telling lies'. Most of our students are bright enough to 'get' the texts. Explaining large chunks is usually unnecessary, especially if we use matrices judiciously. What our students most struggle with is naming and explaining these ideas.

I'd also confused intelligence with memory. Many of my students find remembering information difficult but they are very perceptive. This led me to create a lexicon to help them express their ideas. It had to be flexible enough to apply to a range of seen and unseen texts, so that the words would link to the common concepts and attributes of literature. I realised that we need high-leverage words, and it can be effective to teach them in binary pairs. This also helps students to spot how other writers use opposites (conflict!) to create meaning.

HOW?

These are the pairs of 'buzzwords' that I teach my students:

Turbulent	Placid
Dionysian	Apollonian
Frustrated	Stimulated
Resentful	Satisfied
Dystopian	Utopian
Pessimistic	Optimistic
Resistant	Acquiescent
Innocent	Experienced

Beware students assuming that these pairs are the dreaded 'positive' and 'negative'. Students should be aware that their use very much depends on the context. An acquiescent character might be desirable or not depending on what they're giving in to!

These buzzwords are high leverage because we can use them to satisfy AO1 and AO2. For example:

- *'Macbeth's turbulence is evident in his witnessing Banquo's resentful ghost.'* (AO1)

- *'The turbulent paradox 'fair is foul' indicates a newly emerging moral relativism.'* (AO2/AO3)

The words can be used to describe characters and events but also the effects of language, so students do not need to rote-learn endless lists of adjectives. We can also go back to our matrices and link these words to them. For example, I might say the time motif is a sign of Macbeth's *frustration* because he doesn't have an heir. This makes him *resentful* of Banquo. I'm again linking this new knowledge to our existing schemas.

There are a few more buzzwords that can also liven up discussions of ideology:

Conservative	Subversive
Traditional	Radical
Disenfranchised	Franchised
Powerful	Powerless
Superior	Inferior
Taboo	Permitted

This lexis can be linked to the big ideas. For instance, one can be politically, morally and culturally frustrated. Below is an example of how we can use a limited lexicon to sharpen inference, explain the effects of language and define the big ideas the writer is steering us towards.

Macduff is a man resentful of Macbeth's Dionysian transgressions; Macbeth's resistance of the system has resulted in the breaking of the worst taboos, showing us the value of social hierarchy. Employing the alarming motif of blood reinforces the turbulence Macbeth has created in his society. It's as if the subversive Macbeth has slaughtered social order itself as well as Macduff's family.

LEARNING THE BUZZWORDS

We know that students need to develop their vocabulary to respond meaningfully to texts and to express their own ideas with distinction, but how can we make sure they can use this vocabulary fluently?

Learning words in isolation with the look-cover-write-check method has limited results. It seems to imply that vocabulary runs alongside what we do as critics and writers, instead of it being a driving force. It's also time-consuming.

The education researcher Timothy Shenahan recommends in his blog that students need to have a new word repeated 10–15 times in order to learn it. However, we would hope that by revisiting and interleaving topics, we would display the vocabulary many more times than this. Certainly, we should plan when we'll teach, re-teach and consolidate the technical language of our topics, but teaching isn't a guarantee of learning.

When it comes to teaching the buzzwords, some effective methods for me have been:

- Explicitly teaching a pair of words in the opening of the lesson. If I'm going to focus on the matrix of villainy in *Othello*, I might open the lesson with an exploration of 'resentful' and 'satisfied'. Remember, we're learning how the words link to literature, so don't settle for general definitions from students. I would break the word into its morphemes (the individual units of meaning). That is, the prefix 'satis' means 'enough'. I would also talk a little about the etymology or origin of the word. For example, 'resentful' comes from a phrase meaning 'to be oppressed'. With this knowledge, the words are not seen as random shapes and students can see the logic in the unfamiliar. Many teachers recommend an etymological approach but in the past I've always had to cut back on this because of wading through texts, despite knowing it to be effective. Reducing texts with matrices has left me time to explicitly teach the vocabulary that will enable students to make sense of their responses.

- Giving a pair of words to a small group of students for homework. They report back on the pair.

- Creating a lexicon in the back of students' books so they can refer to it.

- Linking the words back to the matrices.

- Defining chapters and scenes with the words.

- Ranking the words in order of relevance for the different texts.

- Writing thumbnail sketches of an 'Apollonian' character or an 'innocent' landscape so that students think more creatively about the definitions.

- Using the words when cold reading. Is the tone of the extract Apollonian? Is the opening utopian?

- Linking the words to 'Archetype guess who' (page 37). Could a sage ever be acquiescent? How might an ingénue feel disenfranchised?

- Linking the words to 'The four humours' (page 38). How might someone who's phlegmatic also be Apollonian?

- Debating which words different characters would apply to each other.

- Opposing the words against each other to explore how they might present conflict in a text. For example, how would experience be in conflict with innocence? In what scenarios would this manifest? Would they have anything in common? Whose side is the writer mostly on?

- Applying the words whilst using Labov's narrative model. For example, when orienting the text, which word would describe the setting? The first character we're introduced to?

Maximilian Riesenhuber's research from 2015 suggests that seeing new words is more important than hearing them, as the brain stores an image of the word.[25] Activating the image creates automaticity in a way that sounding it out doesn't. This means we can format how we display the word to ease recall, using colours, fonts and graphics to illustrate the meaning of the word visually. And we can increase students' exposure to these high-level words by using them across all the texts.

Figure 14 gives some suggested visualisations of the key words, which we can use to build on our students' pictorial dictionaries. The illustrations aim not just to improve memorisation of the word itself but it's meaning too. Because the buzzwords are presented in pairs, it's simple to create an opposing image. Don't forget to keep showing the word in this format to strengthen recall.

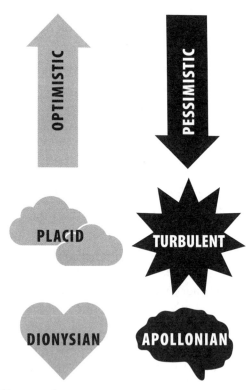

Figure 14: Visual buzzwords

25. Reported in Parks, A. (2015) 'Your Brain Learns New Words by Seeing Them Not Hearing Them', *Time Magazine*.

As can be seen in Figure 15, these words can be incorporated into plot recall. They could be used in character profiles and included in the success criteria of narratives and rhetoric. Multiple exposures such as these will help to strengthen students' understanding of the words.

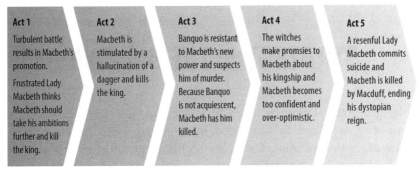

Act 1	Act 2	Act 3	Act 4	Act 5
Turbulent battle results in Macbeth's promotion. Frustrated Lady Macbeth thinks Macbeth should take his ambitions further and kill the king.	Macbeth is stimulated by a hallucination of a dagger and kills the king.	Banquo is resistant to Macbeth's new power and suspects him of murder. Because Banquo is not acquiescent, Macbeth has him killed.	The witches make promsies to Macbeth about his kingship and Macbeth becomes too confident and over-optimistic.	A resenful Lady Macbeth commits suicide and Macbeth is killed by Macduff, ending his dystopian reign.

Figure 15: Plot recall

WHY?

We can't expect our students to be experts in other people's words if we don't furnish them with the best ones too. It's immoral to show students the best writing without gifting them the tools to not only comprehend great writing but to express themselves with greatness too.

Strategy 4: Buzzwords		
What?	**How?**	**Why?**
• Teach students around **20 words** that will describe a range of texts/ ideas.	• Pre-teach vocabulary. • Use as recall starters and interleave throughout an SOW. • Plan each SOW to include regular retrieval and use of the vocabulary. • Support with a knowledge organiser. • Use during cold/hot reading strategies. • Match to episodes from the plot. • Match to characters. • Combine with the language matrices.	• Any text is concerned with ideas of gender, race, class and forms of power and conflict – it's what it's there for! (AO3) • Reduces cognitive load and 'single use' terms (AO1). • Supports memory better. • Provides a lexicon for unseen texts (AO1/3). • Embeds prior knowledge to build textual understanding (schemas) (AO1).

STRATEGY 5: THE BIG FIVE

I like grammar. I even read about it for fun. But I'm aware I'm in a minority. It's hard to keep students engaged when instructing on grammar, but more importantly, it's highly time-consuming: there are few shortcuts to mastery of grammar. In fact, some shortcuts only store up trouble for later. (Yes, I'm looking at you, 'ly word'.) But students do need to discuss language and without labels this can become convoluted.

WHAT?

The Big Five are the most useful language features for students to learn. They are guaranteed to be plentiful in all texts and are relatively easy to identify – students frequently misname adjectives, verbs and adverbs but I don't encounter mistakes with symbols, motifs or of course, lexis. The Big Five are collected in the table below. (Before introducing them, make sure students are aware they will only begin to identify language as they move into hot reading – they still need to make sure they understand the text overall first.)

Technique	Explanation
Lexis/diction (We could also try to sneak in 'semantic field' – a group of words with thematic links.)	Words.
Phrase	Group of words.
Symbol	Represents an idea, character, feeling, etc.
Metaphor	An analogy – similes, personification, etc. are sub-groups of metaphors. We can link this to symbolism too.
Motif	Repeated image or idea, etc.

The Big Five are invaluable because they will apply to poetry, prose, drama and non-fiction texts; they will also recur frequently even when texts have been reduced to matrices. These techniques make students comment in greater detail because they mostly come from macro features – that is, language features whose significance goes beyond a single word in a single sentence. Being able to identify a verb correctly isn't really going to improve language analysis in the same way as thoroughly exploring the Big Five.

Having said that, knowledge of the basic building blocks of syntax is important, for example for helping students to understand the different types of phrases to employ in their own writing. If your students need further support with these parts of speech, then use the quick guide in the table below.

Word class	Explanation	Example	Quick tip
Noun	A word that gives a name to a thing. (Noun even sounds like name!)	'Is this a **dagger** which I see before me…' (*Macbeth*)	Can you put 'a' or 'the' in front of the word? Then you have a (common) noun.
Verb	An action or state of being. (Something you can do or be.)	'I will **honour** Christmas in my heart.' (*A Christmas Carol*)	Can you add 'ing' or 'ed' to the word? Then you have a verb.
Adjective	Describes the noun or thing.	'the **patriotic** tear' ('Bayonet Charge')	Can you put 'seems' in front of the word? Then you have an adjective.
Adverb	Describes the verb. (It's even got verb in it!)	'Slowly, Brian nods.' (Stage direction from DNA)	Does the word answer where, when or how? Then you have an adverb.

HOW?

We've seen how the matrix method already prepares students to distinguish and discuss motifs and symbols in particular. Students should be aware that writers will repeat images to convey their ideas, but they need a method to help them explore a range of features and the ways they might link together. 'Biggest–big–small' has proven very helpful for me in the past.

BIGGEST–BIG–SMALL

The 'Biggest–big–small' approach ensures students look more deeply at quotations and go beyond merely classifying a feature. All of us will have seen students write answers like 'The writer uses an adjective to show Hyde is ugly', without an explanation of *why* the writer imparts this detail. Then the teacher might 'correct' the work and advise the student to analyse a broader range of language features (this is certainly the most frequent comment I make on students' work). It's the beginning of good advice but needs to be supported by a method for how to do this. Instil the 'Biggest–big–small' approach and students will have a strategy to follow so they can act on this feedback quickly.

Step 1: Students find a *large* language feature, such as an extended metaphor or motif – techniques that recur in different quotations in the text, extract or matrix. This means multiple quotations are used to support their inferences, which makes them more inclined to comment in more detail. For example, students might be asked to explain how love is presented in *Romeo and Juliet*. They could find two or more quotations where love is used a symbol for freedom or rebellion, etc. Using more than one quotation also encourages students to comment on how the image might have developed or changed throughout the text. (If your classes find language analysis especially tricky, they can apply this to single quotations first to build confidence.)

Here are my chosen quotations from *Romeo and Juliet*:[26]

'With love's light wings did I o'erperch these walls,
For stony limits cannot hold love out.' (Romeo)

'O me, what fray was here?
Yet tell me not, for I have heard it all.
Here's much to do with hate, but more with love.' (Romeo)

Step 2: Students now move on to find smaller techniques in the quotations. This could be a semantic field, phrase or metaphor/analogy. Here, they might explore the semantic field of being trapped in 'walls', 'stony' and 'limits'. They might comment on how Romeo uses the phrase

---

26. Shakespeare, W. (2008) *Romeo and Juliet*. Oxford School Shakespeare.

'I have heard it all' to show his boredom with the grudge against the Capulets and how love is now more exciting for him.

Step 3: Students find the smallest language feature by looking at individual examples of lexis. They might explain the lexis 'wings' and how Romeo links love to angels and salvation. They might contrast it with the lexis 'walls', showing that love can transcend our physical, mental and societal constraints.

Biggest	Big	Small
Full text/paragraph level	**Sentence level**	**Word level**
(We can also refer to these features as being part of the text's macrostructure)		(We can refer to these as being part of the text's microstructure)
Allegory	Metaphor/analogy	Lexis
Symbolism	Phrase	Adjective
Extended metaphor	Semantic field	Verb
Motifs		
Repetition		

'Biggest–big–small' allows students to demonstrate an understanding of the text as a whole whilst evidencing close reading skills. Once they've made notes on the quotations they can then use the framework as a structure for their essay too, as they move from macro analysis to micro analysis.

Below are two examples, one from *Romeo and Juliet* and one from *Macbeth*. These show that the method helps students to write both simpler and more sophisticated responses. We know answers that have a 'unified concept' at their heart fare better and this method helps students to create and build on a central thesis or idea (as in the *Macbeth* example). However, it's also a logical process that helps students wring the best from their inferences, even when they're quite straightforward (as in the Romeo and Juliet example).

Example One: *Romeo and Juliet.* How does Shakespeare present love?

*Shakespeare uses love as a **symbol** of freedom in the play. Romeo says: 'Here's much to do with hate, but more with love,' and 'With love's light wings did I o'erperch these walls for stony limits cannot hold love out,' to show that he wants to be free of the family feud. The **semantic field** of being trapped is indicated by 'walls' and 'limits' and Romeo believes that love will release him from his family's hold. The **lexis** 'wings' has connotations of angels, making it seem that his love is salvation and will heal the rift.*

Example Two: *Macbeth.* How does Shakespeare present Macbeth's marriage?

*Shakespeare uses the disturbing **motif** of blood imagery throughout the play to **symbolise** that Macbeth's relationship is a parody of the idea that marriage is the building block of civilised society. Macbeth laments 'I am in blood/Stepped in so far', whilst Lady Macbeth demands 'Make thick my blood'. Both characters employing blood as a **metaphor** for their destructive personalities shows their uncanny interdependence, as though violence, as well as blood, flows through their veins and therefore their marriage and legacy. Moreover, the **metaphor** is used to demonstrate both strength and weakness. For Lady Macbeth – a woman desperate to deny her sex – the image of blood coupled with the lexis 'thick' demonstrates her rising above her physical and social weakness and above her 'feminine frailty.' Ironically, her marriage – usually an institution of patriarchal control – allows her ambition to flourish. However, for Macbeth, his confession and the **verb** 'stepped' implies the leaking of his power and his almost drowning in the 'influence' of his wife. Blood stains their thoughts and speech and is a constant reminder of their complicity in a brutal transgression.*

This really helps students to elaborate on AO2, but you might still be concerned about feature spotting at the cost of analysis. This can be improved with the 'Feel–find–name' approach.

FEEL-FIND-NAME

Step One = Feel: Make sure students have a response/opinion on what they've read *first*. This can be revised, developed or even scrapped, but they should really respond to the text/extract/matrix as a whole initially. Writers want to engage holistically, not through filleted paragraphs. That's like trying to imagine a cow by staring at a steak! Let's say that we're exploring how Scrooge is presented in Stave One of *A Christmas Carol*. Often students will dive in, highlighters in hand, and start picking out adjectives. The example below was what I most encountered when I checked on my students' 'annotation':

Bad example: *Oh! But he was a tight-fisted hand at the grind- stone, Scrooge! a squeezing, wrenching, grasping, scraping, clutching, covetous, old sinner! Hard and sharp as flint, from which no steel had ever struck out generous fire; secret, and self-contained, and solitary as an oyster. The cold within him froze his old features, nipped his pointed nose, shrivelled his cheek, stiffened his gait; made his eyes red, his thin lips blue and spoke out shrewdly in his grating voice. A frosty rime was on his head, and on his eyebrows, and his wiry chin. He carried his own low temperature always about with him; he iced his office in the dogdays; and didn't thaw it one degree at Christmas.*

The problem here is that they haven't responded to language in any way other than recognising some words as vaguely connected to Scrooge. They also often energetically highlight the first part but neglect the second half. I ask students not to use highlighters but only pens, and they don't zoom in on individual words yet. They read through first and note down their impressions of Scrooge. They might use 'Follow my leader' (page 33) to say briefly what Scrooge is like, what he seems to be in conflict with, and how the extract doesn't change but repeats his parsimonious and apathetic qualities. They might apply the 'Four Humours' (page 38), commenting on his choleric and melancholic air. They could use 'Buzzwords' (page 81) to note where he seems resentful and pessimistic. Whatever strategy they use, they form an opinion first.

Good example: *Oh! But he was a tight-fisted hand at the grind- stone, Scrooge! a squeezing, wrenching, grasping, scraping, clutching, covetous, old sinner! Hard and sharp as flint, from which no steel had ever struck out generous fire; secret, and self-contained, and solitary as an oyster. The cold within him froze his old features, nipped his pointed nose, shrivelled his cheek, stiffened his gait; made his eyes red, his thin lips blue and spoke out shrewdly in his grating voice. A frosty rime was on his head, and on his eyebrows, and his wiry chin. He carried his own low temperature always about with him; he iced his office in the dogdays; and didn't thaw it one degree at Christmas.*

Scrooge seems like someone who's never satisfied with what he has.

He's isolated but independent.

His personality is like winter – phlegmatic

These are not earth-shattering inferences yet, but they do contain a seed of insight that can be built upon in a way that some highlighted adjectives can't. Students have felt something about the text and are now more likely to care about sharing and explaining their ideas.

Step Two = Find: Once students have an opinion, they can now begin to think about how this has been influenced by the language. For instance, if a student comments that Scrooge is never satisfied, what signifies this? Now they can re-read the text, underlining the quotations like 'wrenching' etc. that connect to this idea. These quotations are linking to a schema they've begun to build (their initial opinion) so they're more likely to make and recall meaningful links across the extract and elsewhere in the text.

Step Three = Name: Lastly, students zoom in on specific language features. (But remember, it is better that students can explain ideas and themes rather than correctly identifying an adverb or determiner. So always keep in mind the larger picture: any specific language analysis should link back to the overall message being explained.)

The 'Biggest–big–small' method can also be applied to the matrices, so for instance students might look at the matrix of 'darkness' in *Macbeth* and note their impression first before delving into the specific effects of different language features.

I feel that as teachers of literature we often get this back to front. How many times have we given a text out and a highlighter with the instruction to annotate it? Annotate what? And why? We're giving students a map but without specifying the destination if we do it this way round. Let students react first. Then they analyse the reaction along with the language.

THE WORD ANALYSIS GRID

If you find that students are struggling to explain language meaningfully then you could use a word analysis grid like the one below to explore thoroughly the most significant lexis in the texts. A word grid elaborates on a connotative approach[27] as it breaks down the ways we perceive language category by category. Students can then use the grid to decide which ideas are most supported in the text and are most relevant to the question being asked.

Below is an example of a completed grid. Here I've explored the word 'sharp' from the *Christmas Carol* extract above. We can see that alternative inferences begin to present themselves. Is Scrooge entirely bad? Might he actually be quite insightful about the society he's in? Is he a honed tool for Dickens to tear open society and display its faults to us? There's potential to build a very detailed analysis around a single word in this way.

---

27. The connotative approach means students consider the connotations of diction, so they might say red connotes danger, love etc. The problem with this is that sometimes the connotations don't match. Is love dangerous per se? Sometimes, students just list associations and don't consider which connotations support the writer's ideas.

Is the word...						
Polysemous (more than one meaning)?	Controversial/ Emotive? Or neutral	Literal or metaphorical?	Technical?	Formal or informal?	Euphemistic or taboo?	Ambiguous?
• Thin edge • Clever • Pointed • Critical • Rude Sharp can apply to people and objects.	Blades, weapons but could be desirable if we're talking about intelligence.	Metaphor – a person can be sharp beacuse they might cut like an edge.	Could be used to describe certain tools and machines.	Formal.	Can be a compliment when linked to intelligence but insulting when linked to behaviour.	IS Scrooge: Harmful? Clever? Useful?

I've used students' word grids as the content for model responses and this has been especially effective. Students are no longer following the inferential train of thought, as this has already been laid out to them, but instead are focusing on how I *explain* the inferences, employ a range of phrases to clarify and elaborate, and use connectives to present multiple ideas.

WHY?

The report *Learning: What is it and How Might We Catalyse It* says we can only attend to a few things at once. If students are too busy trying to work out the word class, this can mean they forget that they need to explain the effects of the language. As we've seen before, limiting the tools a student uses means they have to employ those few tools with greater precision and imagination.

Strategy 5: The Big Five (focusing on five linguistic features)		
What?	How?	Why?
• Students practise their understanding of **five linguistic features**: lexis, phrase, symbol, metaphor and motif (and semantic field added for luck!).	• **Bin highlighters**! • Use **cold and hot reading** to move from comprehension to analysis. • Apply **biggest–big–small** to examine how language adds to meaning of the whole text as well as specific parts. • Use **feel–find–name** so that students respond to the text first and then work backwards to explain their response. • Use the **word analysis grid**. • Employ these techniques in **seen and unseen texts**.	• Prevents pointless feature spotting! • Embeds understanding of language and structure (AO2). • Reduces cognitive load and demands on memory • Links back to the matrix approach (AO1/2/3).

STRATEGY 6: SPACED LEARNING

WHAT?

At its simplest, spaced learning is a code for retrieval. It's a way to replicate the movement of knowledge from short- to long-term memory, and it utilises forgetting to increase memory strength.

Spaced learning is not the same as spaced practice. Spaced practice means that gaps are left between learning episodes before content is revisited. These gaps aren't so long that content is completely forgotten, but aren't so short that students are constantly revising it. This is an effective way to plan and deliver, but we need students to be *introduced* to core content first in order to space it across the SOW and later in the year. Spaced learning is a structure that will more often be used in a distinct lesson, frequently at the beginning of topics. The principle is similar: both approaches recognise the need to strengthen recall by allowing students to forget, but spaced learning plans for this to occur in a single learning episode.

The pioneering research of R Douglas Fields indicates that leaving short gaps between information inputs and retrieval increases later recall.[28] Paul Kelly used this to develop the spaced learning method.[29] This condenses content and introduces the core information in one session so that students can draw upon it in further lessons. This means that instruction is minimised, meaning application and practice can be increased.

28. Fields, R. D. (2005) 'Making Memories Stick', *Scientific American*.
29. Kelley, P. (2007) *Making Minds*. London: Routledge.

Kelley's findings showed that 'learning at a greatly increased speed and in a pattern that included deliberate distraction produced significantly higher scores than random answers'.[30] In short, the method resulted in better exam performance.

Admittedly, spaced learning can seem strange. It goes against our teacher training in many ways because the sessions involve our students, in part, *doing no conscious learning at all.* However, if we make students recall and apply knowledge solidly for an hour or so, it's much more likely to be forgotten when they leave the classroom. This occurs because the knowledge does not have an opportunity to move from their working memory into their long-term memory. I'm confident many of you will have enjoyed fantastic lessons with students on a Thursday but when they came in on Monday it was as if it hadn't happened!

I was introduced to spaced learning by Emma Lamey when I was a trainee in a placement school. As she explained the process, I felt a tremor of panic and excitement. On the one hand, it flew in the face of much of what I'd been advised; on the other hand, it was logical and potentially transformative. She explained how she'd used spaced learning to introduce the plot and themes of *King Lear* and showed me her students' books. Perfect plot summaries and character profiles filled the pages. These were followed by paragraphs of close analysis. They were Year 7 students.

Not only did this moment inspire me to change some of my teaching methods, but it made me a convert to educational research. Previously, it felt like I didn't have time to read research as I was too busy getting on with the job. After this, it was as if I didn't have time *not* to keep up with research.

Since being a trainee, I've used spaced learning with classes of all abilities at the opening of topics and for revision sessions. One Year 8 class grasped *The Taming of the Shrew* so quickly that I had to re-plan the SOW so that it incorporated literary theory. Students were no longer spending a lesson trying to figure out how many suitors Bianca has but were able to explore

---

30. Kelley, P. (2015) 'Making long-term memories in minutes: a spaced learning pattern from memory research in education', *Human Neuroscience.*

how Shakespeare employed stichomythia to demonstrate power games between the sexes!

It's also telling that many of the methods I used as a trainee have since been dropped – except for spaced learning or metacognition.

HOW?

Teachers present 'input' sessions; students merely listen to these inputs. It does help if you practise this and make the mini-lecture as interesting as possible – but don't make them too flashy! This will take their attention away from the core content.

Then comes the space. Students complete an entirely unrelated task so they can let the original information move from their working memory to their long-term memory. This is where teachers get nervous. You might be wondering how I can promote 'filler tasks' in a book about speeding up progress and saving time. But this 'space' is how students forget the information so they recall it later on in the lesson and will be better able to recollect it further on in the SOW. If they complete a task that in any way links to the content, they're keeping the information in their working memory. Also, this would turn it into a 'normal' lesson: that is, the teacher informs and the students immediately use the information in some way. There's a place for this but not in a spaced learning session (because then it wouldn't be a spaced learning session of course!).

Next, there is another short input that briefly recaps the original information, before a task that calls for students' recall and application of this information. This is followed by another unrelated task and then a final short input and recall/application task.

I use the technique to introduce new topics and to revise old ones, but it's helped when new students have joined my classes too. I once had a group of EAL learners join my class in Year 11. This was difficult because my original class had completed early entry Literature and were now focused on the Language exam, whereas the new students still hadn't sat their Literature papers. Spaced learning allowed me to teach the texts quickly and in the same lesson as the other students. I could set the Language students to work on a narrative whilst conducting a spaced learning session for the other group. I'm not sure how I would have caught these students up without the technique. Additionally, if you're nervous of skipping some content by focusing on matrices and buzzwords etc., spaced learning is where you can cover some of that.

It's much easier to see a lesson built around this process than to hear it described. Below is an overview of a spaced lesson on *A Christmas Carol* that uses the suggested temporal code of Fields. Before a spaced learning session, I explain to students what will happen and why we're doing something different. Students look forward to the lessons because they don't *seem* to require too much hard work, and they concentrate and behave well as they want to enjoy the space activities.

- **Do now:** Some short recall questions on literature in general. This will activate students' existing schemas, giving them a framework for the new knowledge.

- **Input 1:** Students listen to a 10-minute talk that recaps the plot, themes and techniques of the novella. They don't take notes but must listen attentively. Warn students that they will be quizzed later!

- **Space 1:** Students make snowflakes for 10 to 15 minutes. This task uses motor rather than linguistic skills so doesn't rely on any of the knowledge or skills from the input. This means the original information is no longer in their working memory. Don't be tempted to sneak in a task about a different topic because students will use skills too similar to the ones they're supposed to be forgetting! I like the space activities because I can chat to students during them. Don't talk about the learning; keep it as chit-chat to build relationships and to help you keep an eye on vulnerable students.

- **Short input:** The core information is reiterated briefly.

- **Recall task 1:** Students complete a multiple choice quiz on the content.

- **Space 2:** Students colour in a pattern for 10 to 15 minutes.

- **Short input:** Reiterate the core information once more.

- **Recall task 2:** Students complete a matching task linking characters to attributes, quotations and themes. An exit ticket[31] can be included at the end of the session so that you can keep track of what has been understood.

WHY?

The shortcomings of this approach seem obvious – it relies on students listening attentively; it incorporates irrelevant tasks; and it could look strange to classroom visitors. But don't underestimate students! Outlining why the lesson follows a different format is enough to get them on board. Signal that the space tasks are over with a clear 'Everyone looking at me,' and refuse to move to the inputs until this happens.

Truthfully, spaced learning was not popular when I first used it. However, its outcomes were popular. I can assure you that after using this method, I spent little time correcting plot and character mistakes and could increase the complexity of the knowledge each time I returned to the content. I could also employ the matrices quickly because students were secure on plot. Using the matrices then meant that students were analysing the text as a whole within a session or two. Without spaced learning, some of my classes would have still been completing plot summaries at this point.

You can also use spaced learning to introduce the idea of cold and hot reading. It can be employed to instruct on skills and strategies as well as content: I've used it to teach the basics of narrative and rhetorical writing. Whatever your students need to know, it can be introduced effectively in this way.

I'll admit that for students who have memory difficulties it hasn't been as efficacious. Nonetheless, it does provide some background knowledge

---

31. Exit tickets are a type of formative assessment that students complete at the end of a lesson. Sometimes exit tickets are misunderstood as teachers think the point is simply that they have to be completed before a student leaves. Their actual purpose is to assess if students have learnt the main lesson objective. Teachers can then look at a random sample, or a representative sample from most and least able, to identify misconceptions and to guide them in what they will teach next. An exit ticket can be as simple as one key question or might contain multiple choice questions.

for them to build on. Promising a spaced session towards the end of term and in occasional revision sessions banks goodwill too and lets me ease up on the early entry students. I work them very hard, but these sessions give me time to connect with them as people and not just as students.

In the Introduction, I expressed my concerns about how we can provide emotional support as well as rigorous exam training. Spaced learning helps with this. When I detected one of my groups becoming jaded and restless with A Christmas Carol, I dressed as The Ghost of Exams Yet to Come and delivered a spaced learning session in character. A bit of a gimmick, yes, but if we plan to use the most efficient teaching and learning methods well, then there will be time to be playful and link back to why we're studying literature in the first place – because it's subversive!

Strategy 6: Spaced learning		
What?	**How?**	**Why?**
A method of **inputting core content in three blocks** with **short intervals in between**, where students engage in unrelated activities (space activities).	• Teacher delivers **core content** in a ten-minute lecture; students then take part in a **spaced activity**; this is followed by a **shorter input** from the teacher with students using this information in a **practice activity**; students undertake a **second spaced activity**; students receive a final input and complete a **second practice task**. • Use at the start of SOWs for best results. • Combine with interleaving and retrieval practice.	• Core content can be reduced significantly. • Time can be spent on using the knowledge, not wading through content. • The approach replicates the movement of learning from short-term to long-term memory. • The 'forgetting' process strengthens memory. • The sessions can introduce or consolidate knowledge. • The structure is great for revision and provides a revision format for students to use independently. • Plot, themes, techniques and content can be taught simultaneously, proving that they are inextricable (AO1/2/3). • The spaces allow for conversation with students that don't solely revolve around learning.

STRATEGY 7: METACOGNITION IS YOUR FRIEND!

WHAT?

Metacognition is not well liked. Many teachers seem to be suspicious of the word. But let's rename it. We could just call it: teaching. For me, no effective teacher can teach without doing so metacognitively. Good teachers know:

1. Students must be informed of what they're learning and why they're learning it. (*What* to think about.)

2. They need strategies to understand, remember and refine what they're learning. (*How* to think about it.)

3. These strategies should lead to students eventually becoming autonomous learners because they'll know which strategies help them the most. (*Why* they're thinking about it in that way.)

The Education Endowment Foundation's report *Metacognition and Self-Regulation: Evidence Review* states:

On average, intelligence uniquely accounts for 10% of variance in learning, metacognitive skills uniquely account for 17% of the variance, whereas both predictors together share another 20% of variance in learning for students of different ages and background, for different types of tasks, and for different domains. The implication, according to Veenman et al (2006), is that an adequate level of metacognition may compensate for students' cognitive limitations.[32]

This is excellent news as we have a method that can help students achieve more equally. We also know that we don't need to over-differentiate in order to improve students' outcomes. Furthermore, in *What Works*, researchers reveal that up to *seven months* of progress was gained through the explicit teaching of metacognitive strategies. Their studies also support the idea that metacognition especially boosts the performance of lower attainers. This is really important to be aware of because some teachers feel that discussion of learning strategies is somehow 'higher order'. I employ the metacognitive strategies in this chapter with students of all abilities and improvements have been apparent across the board.

Fundamentally, metacognition is being aware of one's own thoughts – what they are, how they've been imparted, how they might need to develop, how they can be used to problem solve. If a student is metacognitive, they will know which strategy to employ to hone which skill. This is a code for achievement. No matter how talented or competent a student might be, they can't move towards mastery without adjusting their practice.

When time and patience are short, it can be tempting to have students repeat tasks and con ourselves that this means they will get better. Repeated practice will only work if students know how to apply and adapt practice at each turn. That's metacognition. Moreover, marking work and giving feedback is pointless too if students haven't been prepared on how to improve. Whilst I sympathise with an aversion to jargon, I also know that a focus on metacognition has meant the basics of teaching remain at the forefront of my practice. No matter what trends schools/OFSTED/ DoE wants. Metacognition is the basis of what we do. And whilst you might not immediately agree, it's refreshingly, wonderfully simple!

Before planning and delivering you need to: ascertain the best knowledge and skills, assign some strategies, some opportunities for modelling and practice, and time for evaluation of these strategies. There's no need to

---

32. Muijs, D. and Bokhove, C. (2020) *Metacognition and Self-Regulation: Evidence Review*. London: Education Endowment Foundation.

delve into VAK, experiential chaos, dressing up, mad tasks, increasing so-called engagement... metacognition allows us to teach and not entertain students; it is equipping students to understand how they can best learn knowledge and skills. Appealingly, considering the strategies your students will need is the bulk of your planning. Think: What do your students need to learn most? What strategies will help them to learn and apply this? This means the need for resources and worksheets can be reduced drastically. This must convince metacognitive sceptics, surely!

HOW?

Metacognition is much easier to utilise than to proselytise about.

A metacognitive approach would be:

1. Tell students what they will learn and why they're learning it (Strategy 1 – 'Reading is Rebellion' –supports this.)

2. Show them strategies for learning (such as 'Cold and Hot Reading' – Strategy 2).

3. Allow students to practise these strategies.

4. Discuss and evaluate the strategies.

5. Amend strategies as needed.

6. Allow students to choose and use strategies independently.

At the beginning of the year, I deliver some general lessons outlining the cold and hot reading strategies, then I add to these throughout the topics as we develop and amend. A good way to introduce the cold and hot reading strategies is to apply them to short unseen poems. I talk students through the reading continuum, outline some reading strategies, then let them apply them. We'll discuss what has been most effective and what we'll tweak when we use them again.

During lockdown, I was exploring an unseen poem with a group remotely. I asked them to recount some hot reading strategies that might help us on our re-reads. A student commented that she searched for opposite words. This wasn't one of our 'official' strategies but she demonstrated how it helped her so we added it to our strategy menu. We also discussed how it linked to 'Who vs. Who' (see page 35). The student demonstrated metacognition because she was aware of the problem and ways she'd solved it before.

When I know my students have some awareness of reading strategies, I can plan more specifically for individual texts. The table below gives one of my learning overviews for teaching *Macbeth* for the first time. I stick to this knowledge and skills in my planning, albeit moving slower or faster depending on needs. In the 'evidence' column, students add the date they produced work that focused on this skill, so we can refer back for examples. Either myself, the student or a peer will add a target, as well as suggest a strategy to help meet or even exceed this target. In this way, we're not going to be distracted from the core knowledge and supporting strategies. At the start of the SOW, I share this information with students and make it plain that these objectives will be revisited and developed.

I will learn...	Evidence	Target	Strategy	Task
the ingredients of classical tragedy				
how to read a play culturally, sociologically, politically and historically				
the importance of equivocation				
Jacobean attitudes to masculinity				
to write a unified analysis by using a triple thesis statement, embedded quotations and summative comments				
to use rhetoric as a means of close reading				

This approach was adapted during lockdown to provide talented students with a basis for further study through remote learning. It skips any fundamental comprehension or plot recall as students understood this very quickly and through independent tasks. If the basics of the plot and play have already been taught and the focus is now on matrices, more challenging content can be broached.

For each objective in the learning overview, I'll explain what strategies will aid students in meeting their target. Let's take for example 'how to read a play culturally, sociologically, politically and historically'. We'll say the student has written an analysis that's made some inferences and explored the effects of language, but they haven't linked this to the bigger ideas. Their target would be to explicate how their inference links to society. The strategy might be to locate the quotations they've used in specific matrices and check back on the overarching messages, or it might be to re-read the text so they can discover comments on conflict and/or power. They might apply the strategies of 'Who vs who?' (page 35) or 'Power games' (page 43). They might look back at 'Buzzwords' (Strategy 4) to remind them of recurrent attitudes towards social concerns. Their task would then be to continue their analysis, explaining the new big idea. (This task could also be made more specific, for example by asking them to explain the idea using appositive phrases or similar.)

It's apparent that each objective will be supported by a framework, and a great labour-saving device is the 'strategies menu'. This simply collects together the strategies that students have been employing. You can leave space for them to add their own too. The menu can be elaborated or reduced depending on where learners are in the cycle. See Figure 16 for an example.

STRATEGIES MENU

What?	How?	Why?
What themes is the play about?	What lexis/ words/ structural features have made you think this?	Why does the playwright want you to think about these themes?

Biggest	Big	Small
What is the largest language feature you can find? Usually one of: extended metaphor, metaphor, symbol or simile.	This could be a semantic field, imagery, list, juxtaposition, etc.	This would be nouns, verbs, adjectives, adverbs and connotations.

Reading strategies

Imagine it's an allegory; what is the hidden message? Where are the symbols?

What are the conflicts?

Where are the transhistorical ideas?

Parse metaphors into metaphrand, metaphier and paraphrand.

Types of conflict

Person vs another person

Person vs society

Person vs themselves

Person vs nature

Summative paragraph

Don't say 'to conclude' etc. Begin with:
• The reader has been made aware that...
• The play has displayed...
• The character has symbolised...
Use the words from your thesis statement but you might say how their meaning has grown/changed. E.g. 'Masculinity becomes a toxic force in the play, more associated with weakness than strength.'

Still stuck on a thesis statement?

Remember, texts are either celebrating or criticising something – usually criticising it to make us question our ideas. You could begin with: 'The writer criticises the belief(s) that... to make us reconsider...'

Figure 16: Example strategies menu

Students are first coached on the strategies in the menu, then guided to the strategies, and ultimately encouraged to make informed choices for themselves about which strategies to use.

By focusing on the strategies, much less time is spent creating lessons and resources, leaving more energy for the classroom. If you genuinely know what you're teaching, why you're teaching it, and have a secure knowledge of how best to teach it, you can arrive to lessons with the set text, matrix or unseen extract and little else.

Metacognition also speeds up marking because we don't have to write long comments on work. Here's an example from a whole-class feedback sheet. Most classes will require similar support and metacognition allows us to give diagnostic, targeted feedback. We might be able to say what's wrong with a student's work, but this doesn't direct them on how to improve. Embedding metacognitive approaches does.

Group 1	Explain at least three language features per quotation.	• Use **what/how/why** to read texts. • Use **biggest–big–small** to identify language features. • Use the **lexical analysis grid**. • Employ could/might/may to offer more interpretations of the lexis.
Group 2	Craft a triple thesis statement in the opening of your essay.	• Use **what/how/why** to find the superordinate ideas. • Use **transhistorical reading** to identify what makes them a superordinate idea. • Frame your ideas in a **noun phrase**; develop one of them in an **appositive sentence**.

However, if you want to provide even more deeply personalised and diagnostic feedback, try the technique in the table below. I work out the minimum number of marks needed on each question for each student and work out the steps that will take them there. I can also hedge my bets and see where marks can be dropped or gained. Sometimes the strategies to improve are idiosyncratic or developed with the student, but more often than not, they're drawn from our existing menu.

Question	Mock result	Steps to improve	Target for Spring 2	Outcomes
1	3/4	Keep applying RAFT!	4	
2	0/8	Use feel–find–name/5 senses reading strategy. **Write 2 PELS.** Consider semantic field and connotations to bulk out your explanation.	5	
3	1/8	Comment on opening, closing and **changes** in the text. **Write 2 SEE paragraphs. One on opening, one on closing.** Brain train the text.	5	
4	0/20	Use feel–find–name/5 senses reading strategy. Evaluate clearly the effect(s) on the reader. **Write 3 PEL paragraphs** Use part of your answer to question 2 to help. Consider semantic field and connotations.	12	

| 5 | 8/24 content 7/16 SPAG **Total = 19** | Plan! **Content:** Interesting vocab with some use of language features and sentence types (3 per paragraph minimum). Use mimesis. **Organisation:** Some use of structural features (interesting opening, changes, climax). 5 paragraphs. Some use of connectives. | 2/20 12/16 **Total = 50** | |

I've included this example from the Language Papers to show this approach works even when there are a number of different questions to tackle in the exam, as well as to show how many of the Literature strategies are transferable. It looks like a lot of work, but once the format has been established it can be updated quickly, and ultimately ownership should pass to the student.

When students complete formative assessment, I also give them a short form to fill in afterwards to assess their application and evaluation of strategies (see the table below). This will tell me if the student is likely to be able to replicate the outcome of the assessment.

Assessment reflection			
What skills did the assessment test you on?	What strategies did you use to demonstrate these skills?	How would you change these strategies next time?	Can these strategies help you with any other tasks?

This can be adapted so that students fill it in before they begin a task too. You can then check before they begin if they're on the right track.

WHY?

Quite simply, an awareness of metacognition is an awareness of effective teaching. If students are only able to complete tasks with your support, then teaching is happening but learning isn't. Metacognitive approaches unite teaching and learning.

From my own experience, I'm confident that gifting students with a range of strategies is the best way to increase performance. Before the chaos of lockdown, my students took their mock exam in January. They performed well but what cheered me most was that they had written which strategies to use on which question. I felt the results were more indicative because they suggested how students might have performed on other occasions too.

Strategy 7: Metacognition is your friend!		
What?	**How?**	**Why?**
• Teaching students the **best ways to think, learn and problem solve**. • Providing strategies to **solve problems**.	• **Plan problems/strategies** as you develop SOWs. • Create a **learning overview** of the SOW for students that makes knowledge/skills clear. • Develop a **strategies menu** to support students. • **Coach** them in the strategies, then move to **guiding** them to choose strategies. • Enable students to **solve problems independently** with reference to the strategies. • **Interleave** content/strategies. • A **spaced learning** session could be included to introduce the strategies/content.	• Metacognition is teaching and learning! • Teaching strategies more than content is speedier and more transferable learning. • Use or misuse of a strategy is a diagnostic tool that allows for immediate and richer feedback. • Marking is faster and more effective if it's linked to the strategies. • Helps to develop a cohesive curriculum rather than one composed of discrete units. • Reduces planning/resource making. • Enables more independent work and more effective homework/study skills. • Allows for personalised targets to be set quickly.

STRATEGY 8: ANALOGY IS ALL

WHAT?

The problems and conflict in literature are invariant. It's bolstering to think this way when we have so much content to ladle onto our students' plates. Whilst in truth it is a debatable premise, it's not without validity: literature is predictable. Texts will share more patterns than idiosyncrasies and we have to initiate our students into this code for them to become effective literary scholars.

My philosophy is this: once students understand the nature of analogy, they understand literature.

Literature attempts to make the absent present and to concretise the abstract; therefore, all reading is about inference. I hear teachers talking about moving from comprehension to the hallowed skill of inference, but even basic understanding is an act of inference, of interpreting what is included and what's left out. Let's look at an example:

Lewis sat at his desk, chewing his pencil, wishing the bell would ring.

This sentence is not at all complex. Lewis is obviously a schoolboy. Hang on, though. Obviously? Students have to make inferences in order to understand even *explicit* information. The narrative is likely to continue to describe a reluctant schoolboy and students are probably able to deduce his personality and state of mind from his behaviour in the classroom. But the understanding, however basic, is still an inference. We're not *informed* he's at school, or young, or bored. In fact, we're not told he's a he!

What if Lewis is a university student? Someone on a job-seeking course?

Even a teacher stuck in CPD? A skilled writer subverts our immediate inferences often, but relies on us *accepting* what is made present and concrete first. This is why comprehension cannot be underestimated. Let's go back to our reading continuum and make it an inference continuum (see Figure 17). This will again illustrate to our students that the process is never complete and requires different strategies to deepen and enrich their understanding.

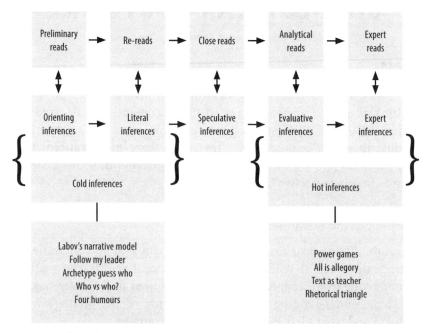

Figure 17: The inference continuum

Figure 17 shows how students need to know that inference has degrees. I'll demonstrate this by exploring the opening of *Jane Eyre*:

There was no possibility of taking a walk that day. We had been wandering, indeed, in the leafless shrubbery an hour in the morning; but since dinner (Mrs. Reed, when there was no company, dined early) the cold winter wind had brought with it clouds so sombre, and a rain so penetrating, that further out-door exercise was now out of the question.[33]

Let's say I've asked students to explain the significance of the setting. The table below shows how we can build on an 'obvious' inference (Jane's not outside) and eventually develop it into an evaluative one (Jane's desires are denied by her environment and by her society).

Inference	Setting
Orienting	Jane is inside. (Note here how much decoding students have to do to come up with what we might dismiss as a self-evident comment. Even though we're told the character won't be going outside, we then get a detailed description of this! This is why students need to follow the steps of the continuum to make sure that the inferences are secure and built incrementally.)
Literal	Jane has been outside but it's too cold now to go out.
Speculative	Why does Jane describe the outside more than the inside? Does her mood match the weather? Does this change in the weather foreshadow a change in her fortunes?
Evaluative	Bronte describes a setting that her character isn't actually occupying to illustrate that Jane is out of place in her family, age and society.
Expert	This idea is heightened when Jane is locked in the Red Room. She feels she's being imprisoned and punished for her individuality. The wintry season suggests the traditional and dispassionate, whereas Jane seems to align herself from the start with summer and passion.

There are cold inferences, meaning students are getting to know the text, and hot inferences, meaning students begin to link their ideas together as they get to know the text more. Bridging the difference rests on deeper knowledge of analogy. Students must understand that text is analogous: it can only ever be *like* the thing it discusses. That is, a room with a desk, bell and boy is analogous to a classroom; *Jane Eyre's* wind and rain is analogous to bad weather. Again, the most basic inference now has potential for exploration. Why would a writer even bother to create a classroom? What bigger ideas must the setting link to?

We need to consider mimesis. This means literature *mimics* real life and aims for verisimilitude through similitude. I have taught students who don't understand why anyone would care about something that isn't true. I've encountered this with autistic students and students in general. And

---

33. Bronte, C. (1992) *Jane Eyre*. Wordsworth Classics.

I have to pause and think: it is sort of silly, isn't it? This make-believe that we esteem? It's even sillier if we don't demonstrate the purpose of fiction and exactly why 'let's pretend' is so highly valued. Literature represents in order to make us think about (mostly) familiar things in a new way. It mimics but doesn't replace the actual, so students need to know the code to access its virtual world. Literature is a simulation; we can only *compare* it to real life. And the most important literary technique is the metaphor.

HOW?

Focusing on figurative language almost ensures deeper analysis and inferences that move on from the middle of the inference continuum (i.e. from literal to speculative). It can be argued that *text itself is a metaphor*; it's emblematic of its themes and ideas, etc. This leads us back to the 'All is allegory' cold reading strategy on page 46. Metaphors allow writers to compare of course, but their use is far richer and more specific. It's not enough to say to students that a metaphor compares one thing to another. What is the point? Couldn't the writer just describe the exact thing they're talking about?

Generally speaking, metaphors can add flavour; orientate a text in an age or place; make the abstract concrete; make the unknown knowable; contribute humour; or influence opinion by creating a sense of pathos, logos or ethos. This sounds an awful lot like the jobs that literature itself does, doesn't it? Metaphors are not only about content but how the content is organised: they are a structural technique to unify and to remind. And that's why we need to teach them more fully. Metaphors are often an ingredient in success criteria or highlighted in copies of poems, but they're rarely *taught* to students.

Firstly, spend some lessons on the idea of text itself as metaphor and its endeavours to employ similitude to create verisimilitude. I usually open my lesson on analogy with the following questions:

I need to describe a thingymibobbit to a group of students.

- *How might an artist solve this problem?*
- *How might a musician solve this problem?*

- *How might an engineer solve this problem?*
- *How might a writer solve this problem?*

Naturally, students will say the artist will show what it looks like, the musician will make a sound like the thingymibobbit and the engineer will create a diagram or blueprint. Things get interesting when we move on to the writer. Students often say writers show what things look like or recreate their sounds. I ask but how can they show? Can they draw an image? Bang a drum? Often students will begin to discuss an appeal to the five senses; many begin to mention similes and metaphors.

I then read a short description of the thingymibobbit. I ask students to draw what they think this looks like. Invariably, there will be some similarities but also differences between them. Then there's the big reveal: I show them the 'true' image of the thingymibobbit. Again, it has something in common with the students' work but has variations too. Students realise that writers can only ever guide their reader to create the right sort of mental models. So the problem is, how can writers best convey ideas to the reader?

We now discuss the nature of analogy. I'll present a definition, the etymology and an example:

ANALOGY

A comparison showing similarities; a way to create similitude.

analogia (Greek) = ratio.

analogo = correspondence.

School is like a greenhouse where we're forced to grow.

This is a very useful discussion because students begin to see what is unique about literature. Writers present the images but we have to make the connections between them, so we have to be active and investigative readers. We're not passive receivers of messages; we're partly authors of it. In a sense, the text isn't finished until we've joined the ideas together. I've had some students comment that 'we're reading too much' into a text, but all writers want readers to make connections. For students who find fiction pointless, this can be a revelation. It explains why reading is hard and demands critical thinking. Most importantly, it lets our students know they are part of a dialogue with the writer. Literature means we 'talk' with the distant and the dead. This is exciting! Literature should not be done 'at' students but they should be agents in making meaning. Therefore, literature is meaningful to them.

After we've discussed the definition of analogy and explored an example, I'll give students a problem:

> **PROBLEM**
> How does a historian make us understand the time when machinery developed and people began to work in factories?

Students always identify that this refers to the Industrial Revolution. I'll ask, what is a literal revolution? How can building a factory be a revolution? After talking about this, I'll say, how does the historian make us realise the importance of these events? Students are then cognisant that analogy is how we define our world. (See 'Letter Three: Deep Reading' in Maryanne Wolf's Reader, *Come Home* for an elegant and inspiring exploration of this.)

Literature uses analogy in some special ways, but these simply reflect the ways in which we understand our lives. Making analogies is natural. It's not silly that the writer doesn't 'just say what she means'. The writer makes it *clearer* what they mean by providing a frame of reference. Essentially, even though we do need to think carefully about them, analogies make things easier, not harder, to understand. So if students find an analogy in the text and can make connections between it and the world we live in, they're likely to be effective scholars of literature.

You can continue this session by having students explore a range of analogies – particularly those in the matrices. You could ask students to create their own, but this lesson has worked best for me when it's more discussion-based with the whole class working together.

METAPHORS

When students understand why texts are essentially analogous then we can look more closely at metaphors themselves.

Students need to know that a metaphor is composed of constituents, and the most effective way I've done this is by teaching them Julian Jaynes' metaphor, metaphrand and paraphrand.[34] (Students don't need to learn these labels per se, but exploring these parts has made students' explications of metaphors much richer – even LPA students, who often need *more* literary theory but can be denied it on the grounds of dubious 'differentiation'.)

Firstly, we'll define metaphor itself:

Metaphor: from the Greek word *metaphorá*, meaning 'to transfer', but the prefix 'meta' itself means 'to go beyond'. This is already pushing students to look further than the immediate image. Moreover, 'phor' mean 'to produce'. *A metaphor is a child of another idea; a type of similitude.*

Let's look at a specific example.

Metaphor: Scrooge is as solitary as an oyster.

Metaphier: The explicit images in the metaphor. (A lone man and an oyster.)

Metaphrand: The implicit links between the images being compared. (Scrooge is like an oyster because they are both alone and sealed up. They have hard exteriors, perhaps with something valuable inside.)

Paraphier: The connotations and associations of the two images. Here we can explore the individual words in the image. (What does 'solitary' suggest? Does it imply being cloistered, as in a religious sense? Does it link to prison? 'Oyster' connotes opportunities and hidden riches, but also being seized upon and used in some way.)

Paraphrand: The new links and ideas formed by connecting the images. (How do 'religious' and 'oyster' fit together? Is the pearl a symbol of innate goodness in humans? Is Scrooge someone worth fighting to save? Has anyone ever tried to 'use' Scrooge or exploit him? Might we have some sympathy with him?)

We can see how we've moved from simplistic links and literal inferences to speculative inferences as we've parsed or broken down the metaphor.

---

34. Jaynes, J. (2000) *The Origin of Consciousness.*

'Para' means 'side by side', so we have to consider the new ideas when the images are positioned side by side. Ultimately, the etymology indicates how metaphors should be read and used. It takes their analysis beyond a basic explanation and into looking 'beyond' the primary image; it involves looking at how the similitude is created, but more importantly *why* it is created. It also encourages students to make links to other parts of the text as these metaphors ultimately lie 'side by side'. So we might consider how 'oyster' foreshadows 'as light as a feather'. We've moved from the sea (a low image of hell perhaps?) to a high image of the sky (heaven). This means Scrooge's transformation comes across as even greater.

If the terms above seem off-putting to your students, you could shrink the metaphor to the 'meta' and the 'para' only. I'll use an *Othello* quote here: 'O, beware, my lord, of jealousy; It is the green-ey'd monster.'

Meta: Beyond the image – so the first part of the metaphor takes us out of the text and into another image to help us understand. Here we're imagining a creature with glowing eyes.

Para: Beside/side by side – why the images have been linked. Jealousy means we can't see rationally and will visualise everyone as looking sickly and alien. It will not only make ourselves monstrous but the object of our jealousy too.

This illustrates that a metaphor cannot be explicated by a word or phrase, and makes our matrix quotations work even harder. Conveniently, the knowledge of the 'para' prefix links to 'paragraph' and shows students that ideas need to be beside each other (i.e. a new topic equals a new paragraph). This can help with understanding 'paraphrase' too. Students need to build ideas side by side in analysis, not just briefly paraphrasing a text's meaning.

Texts are meta: they go beyond themselves because they make links to other ideas, so analysis needs to include a focus on the images created by the language and the links to the broader ideas. Without consideration of both, there is no analysis.

Another way to explore metaphor is to teach the term in two halves and build these into a grid, similar to our individual word analysis on page 95. I often employ a grid like the one below to make explicating analogies clearer.

Image (What?)	'My gashes cry for help' – Captain, *Macbeth*.
Literal (What?)	• The Captain has been badly wounded in battle and needs aid. • The battle must have been brutal.
Meta (Beyond – what are we being made to think of outside the text?)	• An image of a speaking wound. • We can hear the voices of other wounded soldiers. • It reminds us how pain distracts us. • It tells us how our own pain tries to send us a message.
Phor (New links – why are we being made to think of this?)	• The man's wound is loud so it can be heard by others, indicating that our suffering cannot be hidden. • Blood is like tears but more easily noticed, so physical pain will receive attention but mental pain may not. • Fighting and conflict infantilise us and return us to a childlike state.
What ideas does the metaphor make present in the text?	• Humans are fragile, even in strongly masculine societies. • It is difficult to ignore the suffering of others. • Violence is honoured and wounds are trophies. • Human nature is violent. • Physical suffering is more acknowledged than mental. • War is regressive.

You can take this further by isolating specific lexis in the analogy and explicating in the word analysis grid too.

Analogies can also be explored through the 'Target practice' technique (see page 14) so that students see clearly how analogies are part of a writer's criticism of societal ideas. Add the contention to the centre of the target, but keep the 'arrows' as analogies only. How do these analogies help the writer to illuminate, attack or validate the idea?

WHY?

This focus on metaphors illustrates that texts use analogy much more deeply than to indicate simply that one thing can be like another thing, and this encourages students to make multiple links between images.

A thorough understanding of metaphor will also apply to similes, personification, pathetic fallacy, etc. as these are sub-types of metaphor.

Often, many class hours are spent drumming these definitions into our students, but metaphor serves all of these.

Metaphor is useful when teaching context too. I was fired to think more deeply about analogies whilst reading about the nineteenth century. I came across an explanation of the term 'Industrial Revolution'. As we've seen, it is of course a *metaphor* informed by the French Revolution.[35] And yet I'd never considered this. Even when we think we're teaching 'context', it is often framed in analogous methods. We are brought back *to language itself* constantly.

With a thorough understanding of metaphor, students will understand how writers create meaning in individual texts, but crucially they will also recognise that text itself is about making analogies. When a student comprehends the central analogies in a text, they understand the text itself.

Strategy 8: All is analogy		
What?	**How?**	**Why?**
• Teach students that texts are essentially analogous – **they can only represent an idea.** • They do this through **links and comparisons within and beyond the text.**	• Teach the **mechanics of metaphor** in a discrete lesson. • **Parse metaphors** into their counterparts. • Use a **metaphor analysis grid**. • Don't waste too much time teaching the **minor differences between simile, personification,** etc. • Analyse key lexis in the **word analysis grid**. • Explore analogies with '**Target practice**' (see page 14).	• An understanding of analogy is an understanding of literature! • It equips students with a range of comprehension and analytical strategies (AO1/2/3). • It returns us to the unique importance of literature – making the absent present; making the old new; making the safe radical.

---

35. Harve, C. and Matthew, H. C. G. (2000) Nineteenth Century Britain. Oxford: Oxford University Press.

TEN QUICK FIXES

Teachers are often told that there are no quick fixes in education. I believe this is only partly true. If this book has done its job, that should already be clear. By laying the groundwork for literacy skills and developing problem-solving abilities with the strategies I've outlined, progress will accelerate.

I come across the same difficulties time and time again in my teaching and I know other teachers find these common too. Therefore, these problems and their quick fixes are outlined in the table below. Some of the fixes use the strategies discussed in the rest of this book and some are simple suggestions.

To paraphrase Gandhi, there is more to learning than simply increasing its speed.[36] But increasing the speed of learning so that life can unfold sounds about right.

---

36. Gandhi is believed to have said: 'There is more to life than simply increasing its speed.'

Problem	Solution
1. Students don't read/answer the question set.	1. Have students rewrite the question as a simple essay title, e.g. 'How is masculinity presented in Macbeth?' becomes *'Macbeth* and masculinity.'
	2. Students must use the topic word of the question (in this case 'masculinity') at least three times per paragraph.
2. Students don't plan their answers.	1. Bill it as pre-writing rather than planning.
	2. Use the triple thesis statement as the plan. That is, students give three ideas on the question's topic in the opening (e.g. *Masculinity is presented as destructive, violent and ultimately insecure*). Students look back to the opening to indicate how their essay must progress.
	3. Teach matrices so that students have a number of big ideas to build their answers around.
3. Students don't discuss language.	1. Use the word analysis grid from Strategy 5 (page 95).
	2. Parse analogies by breaking them into metaphrand, metaphier and paraphrand (page 119).
	3. Teach the 'Big five' (see Strategy 5) and rehearse inferences that reference them. (E.g. what semantic fields are in *Henry V*? What inferences can we make from these? What bigger ideas can we link them to?)
4. Students' essays lack a clear central argument.	1. Students create a statement of intent before writing the essay, e.g. 'I want to show… because… I'll demonstrate this by talking about… By the end of the essay, others will know that…'
	2. Hold students to account: has their essay matched their statement of intent? Use the statement as part of the marking criteria.
5. Students aren't writing introductions/conclusions.	1. Do they really need to write these? Would a topic sentence function best as a concise introduction?
	2. A well-crafted thesis statement linked to the writer's intentions works as an introduction and plan (see problem 2).
	3. Can students end their essay with an apposite quote from the matrix/text itself that sums up their argument?
6. Students get the quotations wrong.	1. Teach quotations that link together, e.g. through the matrix of a specific image/symbol (see Strategy 3).
	2. Prioritise analysis of individual quotations above reading or re-reading the entire text. Encourage students to use motif/symbol etc. to reduce quotations and to help them focus instead on the explanation of effects. E.g. Students might forget exact quotations that include love in *Romeo and Juliet*, but should be able to recall that Romeo repeats this symbol to create a motif suggesting that love is liberating.
	3. Use ellipses (…) to omit the less important diction.

7. Students offer only one interpretation of quotations.	1. Introduce students to parsing (breaking down) metaphors into their constituents (page 119). 2. Make students aware that exam essays are exploratory – it is safe to say might/possibly/potentially, etc. 3. Teach the appositive phrase to offer 'aside' inferences to the main inference in the sentence (page 72).
8. Students name-check many language features without explaining their significance.	1. Apply the 'Biggest–big–small' structure to lexical analysis (page 90). 2. Have students use participial openings to emphasise the effects of language. E.g. *Employing a rueful tone…* (participial openings in this sense are essentially the 'ing' form of verbs). 3. Parse analogies (see Strategy 8). 4. Bin highlighters!
9. Students' answers aren't clear.	1. Increase the use of noun phrases (page 72). 2. Have students explain inferences by adding infinitive verb phrases (page 73). 3. Students create a title for the essay and link all ideas back to it (see problem 1 above).
10. Students' responses are too short/ underdeveloped.	1. Have students link the question to matrices and explore as many themes/ ideas within the matrix as possible. 2. Open with the triple thesis statement. 3. Employ infinitive verb phrases to develop analysis of language (page 73). 4. Parse analogies (see Strategy 8).

GLOSSARY

Apollonian. Rational, organised, disciplined. Originates from Apollo, the God of the sun.

Aporia. Can mean a breakdown in logic but mostly refers to the expression of doubt in literature. Macbeth's dagger soliloquy could be said to embody this. The most famous example is Hamlet's 'To be or not to be' rumination.

Diagnostic. Showing what students do or don't understand – but something is only diagnostic if the teacher then corrects/advises quickly.

Dionysian. Uninhabited, chaotic, self-indulgent. Originates from Dionysus, the God of wine.

Eschatological. This refers to death, judgement and the afterlife. *A Christmas Carol* and *Macbeth* are full of eschatological references and imagery.

Ethos. Part of the rhetorical triangle, referring to the writer showing their personal response to a topic, creating a sense of credibility and trust.

Interleaving. More than one topic is taught/revised at a time. This helps to improve long-term memory and to avoid the 'spiral' curriculum where topics are suddenly dropped and then picked up later. Interleaving can be achieved through recall starter tasks, explicit linking of skills and knowledge across topics, or dividing the learning episode between topics. Admittedly, it is hard to establish and will test your nerve as information becomes mixed, but over time the benefits are clear and automaticity is heightened.

Kairos. Talking about the right issues at the right time in rhetoric.

Logos. Part of the rhetorical triangle, linking to logic and reason. Where the writer proves their opinions, etc.

Metacognition. This is an awareness of one's learning process and of mental strategies to increase the efficacy of learning. Simply, it asks what do I need to learn? What can I do to learn it? What have I done to learn it and do I need to change/adapt this? This needs explicit teaching but will equip students in the long term to work more independently and from a wide range of solutions.

Mimesis. The way a text mimics and interprets the world. Mimetic methods more often illustrate and hint, as opposed to **diegesis** which outlines/informs. These are great terms to help students enrich their own writing. We often speak of showing (mimesis) not telling (diegesis).

Pathos. Part of the rhetorical triangle. Where the writer inspires an emotional response in the reader.

Schema. Theorised by Jean Piaget, schemas are mental frameworks where information is organised. The construction of effective schemas is essential for long-term memory, as old knowledge provides the basis for new knowledge. New knowledge therefore needs to have a clear link or is likely to be forgotten. This can be ameliorated by helping students build new schemas.

Similitude. The state of being similar to something else.

Stichomythia. A technique in drama where characters speak different lines of verse, or two lines of dialogue are given to alternate speakers.

Subordinate/superordinate. Superordinate themes are the most important and overarching ones in the text, whilst subordinate ideas are the themes that emerge because of the primary ones.

Transhistorical. Crossing the boundaries of history; themes that will be found across the ages in most texts.

Verisimilitude. Seeming to be real; resembling reality.

APPENDIX 1: SUGGESTED MATRICES FOR SET POEMS

Below I've reduced the AQA set poems, as well as some examples from other exam boards, to three or four key concepts each. The obvious links are presented in bold; some interesting connections and parallels are underlined. Remember, the exact words don't have to appear in the poems themselves – connected and synonymous lexis can form part of a matrix too.

AQA 'LOVE AND RELATIONSHIPS' CLUSTER

'When We Two Parted': silence, years, **cold** (we)

'Neutral Tones': grey, die, God (we)

'Winter Swans': rain, stilling, wing (we)

'Singh Song': bride, Indian, colours (ve)

'Love's Philosophy': kiss, mingle, me (me/thou)

'The Farmer's Bride': maid, days, brown (she)

'Porphyria's Lover': **storm/rain**, yellow, ties (I/she)

'I Think of Thee': green, tree, twine (I/thee)

'Walking Away': football, scatter, walking (I/you)

'Follower': globed, stumbled, mapping (he/I)

'Mother, Any Distance': measure, floors, fly (you/I)

'Climbing my Grandfather': free, ridge, climbing (I/his)

'Eden Rock': waiting, light, drifted (I/they)

'Before You Were Mine': before, pavement, sparkle (I/you)

'Letters from Yorkshire': digging, **cold**, messages (he/you/me)

These poems can be explored through the use of pronouns as the focus is on relationships. Reducing the poems to pronouns reveals the structures and conflict/consensus within – for example, the formal, remote 'thou' in 'Love's Philosophy' or the change from 'he' to 'you' as the messages are exchanged in 'Letters from Yorkshire'. The repetition of birds and flight imagery and references to the seasons are also frequent.

AQA 'POWER AND CONFLICT' CLUSTER

'Ozymandias': wreck, sand, words

'Storm on the Island': blows, sea, **nothing**

'The Charge of the Light Brigade': **charge**, jaws, glory

'Bayonet Charge': **charge**, rifle, running

'Exposure': **nothing**, winds, dying

'Prelude': her, troubled, pleasure, lake

'Kamikaze': **sea**, fishing, children

'Poppies': spasms, I, **memorial**

'Remains': probably, possibly, we, **blood**

'War Photographer': nightmare, **remembers**, **blood**

'My Last Duchess': look, blush, smile

'London': marks, every, **blood**

'The Emigree': **sunlight**, **memory**, **paper**

'Checking Out Me History': dem, identity, **sunrise**

'Tissue': **paper**, **light**, design

What is surprising in this cluster is how 'The Emigree' – probably one of the less written about poems – manages to have matrices that all connect to the other poems. We can also reduce the poems to a couple of primary colours: red for blood and blush, and yellow from 'Tissue', 'The Emigree' and 'Checking Out Me History', and even the sand of 'Remains' and 'Ozymandias'.

EXAMPLE FROM THE OTHER EXAM BOARDS

'A Poison Tree': friend, foe, day, night

'Morning Song': nakedness, wind, square

'Valentine': onion, light, cling

'Nettles': regiment, blade, pain

'Flag': breeze, cloth, blind

'My First Weeks': breast, milk, paradise

'Manhunt': only, damaged, mine

'She Walks in Beauty': night, light, peace

'The Soldier': foreign, earth, England

'Mametz Wood': bone, earth, mosaic

APPENDIX 2: SUGGESTED OUTLINE FOR TEACHING THE STRATEGIES

This is obviously quite vague but is more to reassure how much we can do in a short span of time. Of course interleaving and metacognition should be employed throughout, but this provides signposts.

Week	Key skills	Strategies	Best text type
1	• Valuing literature • Understanding analogy • Decoding texts	• Reading is rebellion • Buzzwords • Analogy is all • Metacognition • Cold reading	• Unseen poetry • Extracts from set texts to come • Auxiliary articles
2	• Plot recall and formal and thematic understanding of set texts • Understanding language and structure	• Spaced learning • Analogy is all • The big five • The matrix	• Any set text but I find prose better to begin with
3	• Developing personal interpretations • Judiciously employing textual references • Linking to context	• Hot reading • Buzzwords • The matrix • The big five	• Set text matrices and extracts

4	• Understanding language and structure • Writing analytically	• Hot reading • The big five • The matrix	• Set texts but also model answers
5	• Developing analytical writing • Meeting individual targets	• Reading is rebellion • The matrix • Metacognition	• Set texts combined with an unseen poem to check transference of analytical writing skills • Students' answers
6	• Set text general recall • Unifying the skills	• Spaced learning • Cold and hot reading • The matrix • Metacognition	• Exam-style extracts (if relevant)